UEA

Creative Writing Anthology **2011**

Prose,
Life Writing,
Scriptwriting

egg b●x

UEA Creative Writing Anthology 2011
Prose, Life Writing, Scriptwriting

First published by Egg Box Publishing, 2011.

A CIP record for this book is available from the British Library.

UEA Creative Writing Anthology 2011 is typeset in Oranda 10.5pt on 13pt Leading.

Printed and bound by:
The MPG Books Group,
Bodmin and King's Lynn

Designed and typeset by:

Kettle of Fish Design, Norwich
www.kettleoffishdesign.com

Proofread by:
Sarah Gooderson

Distributed by:
Central Books

ISBN:
978-0955939983

Acknowledgements

Thanks to the following for making this anthology possible:

The Malcolm Bradbury Memorial Fund, the Centre for Creative
and Performing Arts at the University of East Anglia and The School
of Literature & Creative Writing at UEA in partnership with
Egg Box Publishing.

We'd also like to thank the following people:

Moniza Alvi, Trezza Azzopardi, Jean Boase-Beier, Amit Chaudhuri,
Andrew Cowan, Giles Foden, Sarah Gooderson, Lavinia Greenlaw,
Rachel Hore, Kathryn Hughes, Michael Lengsfield, Jean McNeil, Natalie
Mitchell, Natalie Orr, Rob Ritchie, Michèle Roberts, Helen Smith, Henry
Sutton, George Szirtes, Val Taylor and Rebecca Wigmore.

Nathan Hamilton at Egg Box Publishing, and Catrin &
Dylan Lloyd-Edwards at Kettle of Fish Design.

Editorial team:

Desmond Avery
Oonagh Barronwell
Dwight Dunston
Tamsin Flower
Anthony Good
Tom Graves
Edwin Kelly
Francesca Kletz
Eugene Noone
Maureen Phillips
Elizabeth Michelle Ruddick
Charlotte Stretch
Rouan Wilsenach

Contents

Life Writing

Scriptwriting

Foreword

by **Louise Doughty**

There is a quote about acting that I think comes from Harrison Ford: 'It's the being famous I get paid for. The acting I would do for free.' I often repeat an adapted version of this quotation at creative writing students: 'A book advance is to compensate you for the horrors of being published. The writing you should do for free.' Most of them look at me as if I am mad.

I can remember feeling that way about being published, that it was all that mattered, that a published author is somehow an entirely different species of homo sapiens from an unpublished one. It was autumn 1986, twenty-five years ago, that I arrived at the UEA campus, fresh-faced, dressed in black, armed only with a vast amount of wilful ambition that far outweighed my modicum of immature talent. I was delighted to have got my place on the course, as were my fellow students, but we were all there for one reason only. We were hoping it would transform us into published authors. Pretty soon, we learnt the sobering truth. The course would not transform us – it would merely provide a little support and guidance while we persisted with the arduous business of transforming ourselves.

One of our number, the Jordanian writer Fadia Faqir, got a publishing deal for her first novel, *Nisanit*, while still on the course. The rest of us finished our year every bit as unpublished as when we started, although we hoped our prose style had improved. The next success was Mark Illis, who got a two-book deal with Bloomsbury not long after completing the course. The most famous graduate of that year is Anne Enright, but even she didn't publish her first book, a collection of short stories, until 1991 and, although we all expected her to win the Man Booker Prize in about ten minutes flat, it actually took her until 2007, the slowcoach. My first novel was published in 1995. Malcolm Bradbury was later kind enough to refer to our year as a vintage year, but I'm not sure he thought that at the time and we certainly didn't.

When you are unpublished, being published (or produced, if you're a playwright or screenwriter) often seems like, as one student of mine put it, 'The dragon's head on the plate.' After I published my first novel, what I loved most was not feeling embarrassed any more when people asked me what I did. It took me about three years to stop simpering when I told them. But plenty of sobering realities await the author who has dreamed for many years about such success, not least economic ones. The average advance for a first novel at the moment is probably around £7,500. That's for a novel that has taken years to write. The occasional bursts of publicity given to writers who trouser six-figure advances mask the sobering truth that, even when you are published or produced, chances are you will still have to supplement your income elsewhere: teaching, journalism, more lucrative forms of writing such as copywriting. Publication also exposes you to public criticism in a way that can be incredibly painful. You think rejection letters are bad. You wait until they are expanded to 800 words and published in a national newspaper for all to see.

So, given that the rewards are so uncertain, why do so many people want to do it? Why did Fadia and Mark and Anne and I gather with six others in Malcolm Bradbury's office all those years ago, each of us having made considerable personal sacrifices in order to attend the course? Why do the new writers in this anthology want to do it? I don't know them personally but I'm going to hazard a guess. They know all about the pitfalls, but the act of creating a fictional world, be it in prose, drama or poetic form, is simply a wonderful, unmatchable privilege. I doubt whether any of the authors you are about to read here are deluded about how hard being a professional writer or trying to be one can be – some of them may well have been at it for years. The money is rubbish, you remain plagued with self-doubt and are routinely mocked in public – but it's a great job and I wouldn't do anything else. There is a fine moment as a published or produced author, and I wish it for everyone in this anthology: it is when a complete stranger writes to you, out of the blue, and says they enjoyed your work. To earn a living (sort of) by making that human connection, through the means of a story you have made up, is a rare pleasure.

So I hope all the writers included here enjoy this bit for what it is. Attending a course such as those at UEA is a sort of dragon's head on a plate, as is publication in this anthology. Many writers become cynical when they are established, and although I understand that, it's a temptation to be resisted. That's one of the reasons why I continue to teach creative writing myself. It is good to be reminded that creating a world with words is a wonderful thing to do, whatever earthly rewards it may bring you. As this year's batch of writers face the big bad world of the marketplace, they will – I hope – feel they have learned much at UEA, much about writing, much about their fellow students and much about themselves. But the most important thing they will have learned or had emphasised is something they probably knew already, that the important thing is the writing itself.

LD

Louise Doughty attended the MA course at UEA from 1986-7 and was taught by Malcolm Bradbury and Angela Carter. Since then, she has published six novels and one work of non-fiction. Her first book, *Crazy Paving*, was shortlisted for four awards including the John Llewellyn Rhys Prize. Her most recent is *Whatever You Love*, which was shortlisted for the Costa Novel Award and nominated for the Orange Prize and a London Book Award. She has also won awards for short stories and radio plays and broadcasts regularly for BBC Radio 4. In 2008, she was a judge for the Man Booker Prize. Her new novel, *Apple Tree Yard*, will be published by Faber & Faber in 2013.

Prose

Introduction by **Andrew Cowan**

Daniel Bennett
Rachel B. Doyle
Ruth Gilligan
Anthony Good
Hannah Harper
Emma Healey
Debra Isaac
Jenny Karlsson
Nadine Karol
Lars Guthorm Kavli
Sarah Lewis-Hammond

Andrew Morwood
Eugene Noone
Tolu Ogunlesi
Nell Pach
Buku Sarkar
Alice Slater
Charlotte Stretch
Catriona Ward
Anna Wood
Wu Xianlin

This has been my seventh year at UEA, and my seventh group of MA students. If I think back to any particular year, I always remember the particulars of that group: who sat where in the workshop, who was working on what, who were friends and who were possibly not, who came to the parties, who still owes me a drink. But every year, the group forms a quite singular whole, with its own distinct personality, its own collective identity, despite the diversity in the students' backgrounds, whether educational, professional or geographical. And this year has been no exception. Our Prose Fiction students have joined us from all parts of Britain (many, inevitably, via London), but also from Northern Ireland and the Republic of Ireland, from Connecticut, Pennsylvania, and New York via Berlin, as well as Calcutta via New York, and from Sweden, Norway, Romania, Nigeria, and China. They will linger in my mind, I think, as one of the cheeriest and most tight-knit groups, who have come as close as any group to fulfilling our best hope for them, which is that they will become each other's best asset, by which I mean each other's most trusted first reader, firmest critic, and strongest support. We select our students with this in mind, and look forward to welcoming not just a group of exceptional writers, but a group of exceptionally generous editors of each other's writing. The assumption is that the quality of their commitment to each other will find its corollary in the quality of the work they produce while they are with us. The writing showcased in this anthology – and, for the first time, on our newly launched website NewWriting.net – offers ample evidence of that quality, and every justification of our faith in them.

AC

Daniel Bennett

A Warrant For Sorry Hawk
An extract from a novel

There's a measure of forgetfulness in every glass but if you need a whole bottle then there ain't never enough. I had plenty of reasons not to sleep at night. Sand Creek was just one, but it didn't touch me then. I gave no more thought to shooting a Graycoat from a quarter mile than cutting down a squaw from a few feet. All those crimes I committed in uniform and there is absolution of a kind in that.

No, it was not on their account that, on the 3rd of January, 1867, the eve of my twenty-fifth birthday, drunker than I'd ever been on Hog Ranch whiskey, I deserted from Camp Cooke and headed out into the wilderness. I didn't imagine the army searching for a ruined soldier and I had no intention of returning. It was my last effort to purge the memory of one Little Long Thigh, for that was how she was called to mock the red branch of her family tree, although her real name was Mary.

Before Camp Cooke but years after I lost Mary, I was part of Governor Evans's regiment under Colonel Chivington. We were formed for the sole purpose of killing Indians but I had no real feelings about it either way. Cheyenne, Arapahos, Sioux or Crow meant as much to me as Yankee or Dixie, Protestant or Catholic. To me, an Indian woman was just a squaw, even though, when the world was still new (eighteen years young to be exact), I knew one who spoke pidgin English and dressed like French girls in magazines. When we danced, my heart raced and, when I held her close, she smelled so good. Whenever she looked at me sideways, my stomach crunched like a tin can left on a fire.

This Mary was the wife of a Mexican three times her age. Together they ran the ranch where we went to play cards and get drunk. I never knew what forced her into such a union but, whatever it was, it didn't sit right with me.

I'd joined the army not long before on a romantic misconception. I was looking for adventure and found boredom and hard labor. It is not in the nature of frontier soldiers to inquire into each other's origins. Instead, they find community in dice, whiskey and each other's dollars. I spent years with some of these men and learned no more about them than the day we met, except which amongst them was the most rotten. If they'd have died, who would I have told? Then again, who would they find to grieve for me?

I was out of place amongst those rough men and they made ill use of a green horn. My ignorance made me feel foolish and girls were amongst the things I was most ignorant about. Being an orphan, not fitting weighs hard on me.

One thing I could do, turned out, was hold my liquor. Better than my fellows and better than that Mexican. I'd watch everyone drop around me. Only Mary outdid me on it. I still had manners in those days, and I was shy, so she took to me. That's when we started dancing – to no music at all but the snores of everyone around us and the wind outside.

We held back so we could have that time alone, and never spoke on it but exchanged looks which was our kind of code. I felt sick in anticipation of those nights, thinking only of them and hardly sleeping. Ain't that something like love? When you can't hardly eat? It never went any further than dancing because I didn't know how to set the thing in motion. She took my holding back for being gentlemanly and it made her like me all the more.

One day, a brute by the name of Parker dropped something so Mary had to bend down to pick it up – all so he could say something against her honor. I threw myself at him and earned a beating for my trouble. Anyway, the Mexican got wind of the cause of the argument and it made him suspicious.

After that, he must've noticed our looking at each other. One night, he stayed sober and only pretended to sleep. All we did was dance but he saw it all. Next night, Mary was nowhere to be seen. So it went for a few days. I was too much a coward to do anything about it.

Then one evening, I drank hard in search of courage. I found it near dawn and snuck away from the barracks. Sun-up over the plains was red as rust and I'm thinking maybe it's calling for blood. I crept up to the window and saw the two of them asleep. Her face was swollen and covered in bruises, her eyes black as tar.

I don't know how long I stood there, or if I made a noise, but she woke and saw me. She smiled. That smile seemed to invite me in and call me to a new life. It had sobriety in it and maybe the sound of children playing. It was the sound of someone next to you in old age who'd care enough to make sure you were still breathing each morning. I should've smashed through that window. We could have been nothing but a dust cloud before that Mexican could reach for his rifle. But I stood there frozen, lingering dumb-eyed like a steer waiting for a bullet. She must've seen right through me because, just before I turned away, the smile fell from her face.

After that, something inside of me turned over. I stayed away and the rest of the boys burned me for it, calling me Drinkswater because they thought I was abstaining. One of them, one I considered a friend, played me like a winning hand. When he got from me what was really wrong, he laughed so hard he nearly choked. Others have gotten on Little Long Thigh's soft side, he said bent double, but he was sure I was the only one that got down to much dancing. I was too foolish, too proud and just too damned young to remember that there wasn't one man amongst this crew that weren't a liar.

You'll think me an animal, and you'd be right. I spent only the bullet in the chamber for her husband but emptied the whole cylinder on Mary and kept pulling the trigger once the ammo was spent. It's took a long time even to be able to say it. It was many years until I even had a nightmare about it but once the stone was rolled back, the light kept pouring in.

He was an old Mexican, and she half redskin, so no one came looking for me. Perhaps I'd have faced court martial if the times hadn't been all chaos. For the very next day, we got our marching orders down to Wilson's Creek, Missouri. There, white men were killing each other.

In '64, I was hunting Graycoats between Denver and the Arkansas River when Colonel Chivington called for reinforcements for his Colorado Volunteers. I had still not shot a man but from a distance. I joined their

Third regiment as it approached Fort Lyon in mid-November. That was the end of one war for me and the start of another.

Chivington's eyes were as red as mine, but what bit at him was deeper than a winter's dose of scurvy. It was under his charms that I first suffered possession by that demon Patriotism, although now I know that it was working on me the moment they put a rifle in my hands. It has taken years to exorcise.

He called us the 'advance guard of civilization' and appealed directly to those of us newly with him – 'once the Confederacy is brought to its knees, a hundred thousand volunteers just like you will push up the Arkansas and the Platte in search of a new future. New mineral wealth is opening up in Montana, Idaho and Arizona and you've earned it. The savage must join us or make way for the stockman and the farmer.'

Whiskey couldn't have made us more drunk than this battle cry of his. The stars were shining in thousands the night we left Fort Lyon on the 29th. We marched all night underneath them until we reached Sand Creek. It was the only real action I ever saw.

The eastern sky was brightening but there was still no sun. We could see the tepees and the lodges where the stream draws a horseshoe in the land. We galloped across the sand flats in the persisting darkness. Later, I spoke to an old brave who survived that day. He said he thought we was shadow people coming up out of the dirt and wondered what we wanted.

Soon, though, the redskins knew well enough what was coming their way. They were running and screaming. I could see Black Kettle holding the pole on which flew Old Glory. They gathered around it, sure it would protect them from us even after we'd opened fire, sure that it must've been some mistake.

Suffice to say, there were half-breeds amongst them that looked just like my Mary. When one came running up to me, blood streaming from a gash in her forehead, all fighting left me like a departing spirit. She collapsed in my arms. Seemed like the chaos raged around us without a thought for who we were. Felt like bullets changed their course. Just before she died, I heard her whisper my name. Of course, such a thing can't be possible.

I felt paralyzed. It was all I could do to blink my eyes. Although I had spilt plenty of blood, all that the officers saw was a choker. After the battle, I was branded a coward. But the army had need of men. With my letters, I might once have made sergeant but not after that. More than soldiers, it needed laborers. And they judge that you needn't be too brave to wield a shovel.

After the Confederacy surrendered, I was employed to fortify our existing camps. Red Cloud and his warriors were itching to try us. We knew peace couldn't hold. There was no buffalo to hunt and the redskins wouldn't settle to farming.

On measly rations and in squalid conditions, we built quarters, bridges and roads. We took leisure in gambling and whoring. The others were struggling against boredom. For me, it was about drinking whiskey until I'd had enough to dull my senses because I kept hearing Mary's voice everywhere I went, smelt her perfume whenever the evening primrose bloomed and saw her on the horizon every sundown amongst the endless scrub to the east.

I grew more and more useless. So they sent me to Camp Cooke, already made obsolete by the ever-moving frontier. And the camp and I decayed together until, one night, I wandered into the wilderness of the Bear Paw Mountains to seek the peace of a sleep unbroken.

The stars were huge above me. There barely seemed a scratch of black beneath. I closed my eyes without a care for opening them again. The Indians say that the Milky Way is a highroad cluttered with the campfires of their ancestors guiding home the spirits of the dead. I wanted those stars to be the last thing that I saw.

But my eyes did open. And I looked up to see buffalo robes and buckskin leggings. Tall red men, hair braided with strips of painted buckskin and feathers on their heads. I think that I laughed. That the law on earth might really have its model in heaven seemed to me hilarious. I expected to lose my scalp …

Daniel Bennett is working on a 19th-Century American Frontier novel and collating his short stories. Daniel was born in Cambridge in 1980 and studied American and English Literature at UEA. He graduated in 2003 and has been working in Environmental Science ever since. He writes whenever he can.

Rachel B. Doyle

Phone World

An extract from a novel

Sheila had promised a judge that if he let her out on parole she would get a decent job, stay away from Oxycontin and other Schedule II narcotics, and start making amends. This was proving harder than she had imagined. It was a recession and employers could take their pick of candidates. No one in Eastern Tennessee – and she'd applied all over – wanted to hire a 38-year-old woman with a drug problem and an armed robbery conviction. Maybe the former could have been overlooked. The latter was a no-go. This seemed slightly unfair: it had only been a Taser. Not even a real gun.

That hadn't mattered at her sentencing and it only earned her disapproving looks when she mentioned it in interviews. 'Weapons are weapons are weapons,' her transition counselor had claimed, smiling patiently. Sheila had stopped trying to explain it. Dutifully, she filled out forms. Then she returned to her friend Pam's sofa to watch her soaps, drink her gin and tonics and wait for her phone to ring.

Before jail, Sheila was pretty in a faded way. Before drugs, she was ravishing. Ravishing overlapped with the drug use for a time but petered out when Sheila graduated from snorting to shooting. Back then she didn't particularly care how her complexion was faring, but now, looking in the mirror, she cared a lot. It would be easier to get hired for a job she had no passion for if her skin and hair looked healthier. Then, employers might assume she at least had a passion for something besides painkillers. Pam, bless her heart, claimed that Sheila was a better hire now than she was before jail.

'People are always saying how hard it is to keep good employees. And they know you can't leave without getting permission from your P.O.,' Pam explained.

'You're right. I'm a dream candidate. And they even get a tax break.'

Finding work was important not only to the judge and her parole officer. Sheila had set it as her own benchmark, telling herself that she needed a job before she could contact her daughter, Marcie. Somehow she wanted to have something to say other than, 'Hey honey, I'm out.' If she were being truthful, which tended to happen between G&T three and G&T five, Sheila would admit that she was afraid that Marcie would reject her.

When Sheila was sent away, her daughter was a rebellious fifteen, with raccoon eyeliner and five or six holes in each ear. She refused to call Sheila 'Mom', and invited her boyfriends over at all hours, some of them closer to Sheila's age than her own. They skulked in through the basement door with 12-packs of cheap beer. Back then, Sheila was generally so out of it that fighting with her hostile daughter seemed like too much trouble, and so she didn't. She instead spent long hours in the bathtub avoiding Marcie and her beaux while staring at the beads of condensation on the ceiling. Last Sheila had heard, Marcie was living with an aunt on her father's side, and not coming home very often.

There had been certain times in jail when she had fantasized that they were best friends who painted each other's nails and talked about boys. But then on visiting day she would look around for her glowering teenage daughter and find only her newly divorced former neighbor, Pam. Pam was a Christian, so she had been willing to let Sheila stay with her once she got out. She was also lonely, so she was only too happy to spend her evenings talking about someone else's problems.

In a county where next-door neighbors were often a five-minute drive away, Sheila was trapped. Her driver's license had been revoked at her sentencing. The walk to her parole officer's downtown office every other Wednesday took her seventy minutes. Once she was there, sweating in the outdated business clothes she had acquired from the Salvation Army, the meetings never took more than fifteen minutes, and always unfolded as if they were following the same script.

Don, looking harried, motioned for her to sit in a chair in front of his overflowing desk. 'Still hunting for a job?' he asked.

'Yeah.'

'Any interviews since we last met?'

'Yeah, one at Montgomery Donuts.'

'How'd it go?'

'Well, the guy was half my age and asked me if I'd been on death row.'

Don took off his glasses and rubbed his temples. 'I suppose most managers don't really know how to interview parolees.'

'Then he asked me how many people I'd killed during the robbery.'

Don sighed and tapped his pencil. 'What did you say?'

'I said, "That's not on my résumé."'

Don looked out the window. Not a good sign. 'So, how'd you leave it?'

'He said they'd call if they needed me.'

'Listen Sheila, I'll be frank. Less than 25 percent of convicted felons are able to find full-time employment in the first few months. You're going to have to put up with some unpleasant questions if you want to crack that statistic. We both know you can, and I have faith that you will.'

'Yep,' Sheila said. That was generally Don's closing spiel. She knew what he was thinking as a postscript, which was that convicts who didn't get hired were three times as likely to return to prison. Sheila got up to leave.

'You should stop by the Phone World on Frazier Avenue. They have a sign in the window that says they're hiring. I would emphasize your retail experience.'

'That's from when I was in high school,' Sheila said.

'See you in two weeks,' Don said, already looking at the next file.

An old man in the waiting room gave Sheila a suspicious look over his walker as she trudged past. He was probably here for selling his pain medication. She wondered if she had ever bought Oxy from him, then tried not to think about it.

The midday sun was hot against Sheila's polyester blazer. She wasn't really in the mood for rejection, but it made more sense to go to Phone World now, while she was already downtown, than it did to drag herself back later. As always, she had printouts of her résumé and a copy of the Work Readiness Certificate she had earned from the transition center in her handbag. As she walked, Sheila repeated interview tips from the booklet they had given her. 'I don't just want to work here, I want to help you grow your business,' she said quietly as she neared the store.

The 'Help Wanted' sign that Don had seen in the window was still there. As she went in, a bell above the door tinkled. Mounted speakers were blaring Taylor Swift. The middle-aged man at the counter had a greasy brown ponytail and one silver hoop in his ear. He looked like he'd rather be swigging bourbon, or listening to Hank Williams Jr.

'Hello. I'm interested in applying for the position in the window.'

'I'm sure you'd look good in the window,' the man, whose nametag said Gary, answered. 'But we're looking for a sales associate.' He grinned.

Sheila laughed weakly. She felt coerced.

'Do you have a résumé with you?'

'I do.' She pulled it out of her handbag.

'All right then, just sit tight. I'm going to go to the stock room to get our management trainee. She'll be interviewing you today under my supervision.'

'Sounds good,' Sheila said, wishing she could camouflage herself among the phones. Most of the store's space was devoted to the complicated-looking gadgets with tiny keypads that Sheila had no idea how to operate. Most confounding was the iPhone. She'd heard of it, but she didn't understand how one could dial it without buttons. That same phone had caused an uproar last year in State, when a sniffer dog smelled its battery inside Wanda Jenkins's mattress. She was put in solitary for a month, and lost all her good-time credits.

Gary reappeared behind the counter, 'We're ready for you.'

Sheila followed him into a room with a worn couch, a small television set and a circular table with four chairs. There was a *Star Trek* calendar on the wall with that day's date already X'd out. He gestured for her to sit in a metal folding chair at the table, while he sat on the sofa. 'She'll be here in a minute,' he said.

Sheila heard a toilet flush, and a few seconds later, a bored-looking girl in tight jeans sauntered into the room. Sheila flinched as she recognized her daughter but forced her lips into a tentative smile. Marcie stopped abruptly on her way to the table. They hadn't seen each other since Marcie walked out during the first recess of Sheila's trial, three years earlier.

'What are you doing here?' Marcie mouthed, while her manager's head was turned.

Gary hadn't noticed anything amiss. 'Here's her résumé,' he said, thrusting it at Marcie, before she took her seat.

'Thank you,' Marcie said slowly. Despite her initial shock, she now sounded composed. Sheila noted with some pleasure that her daughter had given up caking make-up over her sweet freckles. She was proud of Marcie's calmness, but also slightly unnerved by it.

'Thanks for coming in,' Marcie said, not looking at Sheila but scanning her résumé with raised eyebrows.

'Hello,' Sheila said softly.

'Could you tell us a little about yourself?' Marcie began, in what sounded to Sheila like the most apathetic tone she could muster. Gary nodded approvingly.

'Sure. I'm a … ' Sheila's mind went blank. The monologue she had practiced about how she was a hard worker, who was good with people and very organized, hardly seemed appropriate now. 'I'm a … mother.'

'That's interesting,' Marcie said.

Sheila started again. 'I'm a mother who has made many mistakes, but I am looking to change my life and start over, to get my life back on track.'

'And how do you think a job at Phone World will help you accomplish that?'

'Well, I think staying in touch is important. A phone isn't just an appliance. It's a connection.' Immediately she felt her answer was too much or maybe too little.

'Only if you use it,' Marcie said. 'We make most of our money on the calling plans, not the phones.'

'Of course.'

'I see from your application that you've been convicted of a crime. Can you explain that?'

'I'm glad you asked because I want you to feel comfortable … hiring me. It's embarrassing for me to talk about, but I had a substance abuse problem. It affected those that I love most, but did not interfere with my previous jobs.'

'I see. What was your last job, and what was your wage at that job?'

'Sewing uniforms for twenty cents an hour.'

'And your reason for leaving?' Marcie asked.

'I got paroled,' Sheila said.

'What would you do if there were a conflict between you and a supervisor?'

'I would do my best to listen to the supervisor's criticisms, apologize, and then do everything in my power to correct the situation.' She looked imploringly at her daughter, who looked away.

'Thank you for coming in,' said Gary. 'We're glad we had a chance to talk to you. We'll be giving this some thought and will get back to you in a couple of days.'

'No,' Marcie said, to Gary's surprise. 'I think we can give you an answer now.'

Sheila leaned forward.

'I'm sorry, but I just don't see a place for you here.'

The room was silent except for the ticking of the clock and the muffled country ballad emanating from the showroom. Sheila's mind scrambled for something to say. Should she apologize for not calling? Or for being a bad mother? But instead, she stood up, shook Gary's hand and then her daughter's, and said, 'I appreciate your time and your candor. I'll show myself to the door.'

Rachel B. Doyle is working on a comic novel set in the American South. She is a regular contributor to the *New York Times* travel section, and co-authored a cultural history book on the USA that was published by National Geographic in 2009. She was born in Washington D.C. and graduated in 2006 with a degree in journalism and American studies from New York University.

Ruth Gilligan

In the Beginning Was the Word

Exodus

'It's me, Daniel … Daniel Murphy. Your Daniel. Don't you remember?'

But still the old man's eyes didn't even blink, shoved deep into his head like two snowman's lumps of coal. And his face looked melting to match, wrinkles dripping downwards. Come tomorrow, only a puddle would remain.

Daniel stood beside the bed, shoulders knotted forward, feeling far too bloody large for that tiny room. It was an exact clone of all the others he'd passed along the corridor: little allotments of remaining life, each made 'unique' by the half-hearted decorations which looked about as knackered as the residents themselves. But there were no dog-eared posters or grow-your-own-bonsai trees in here, only books. Hundreds of them. Piled high on every shelf and in each spare corner – even the window ledge – blocking the Wicklow view with words instead.

But not one was spoken.

'Well if you've nothing to say, never mind, so.'

The door slammed behind Daniel louder than he'd meant. The gust of air sent the pages all whispering farewell. The old eyes watched him go, feeling the books' breath upon them, and then, at last, they blinked.

Daniel strode away, past the common room, where shrivelled bodies hunched towards muted TVs, kippot covering the men's bald patches like dodgy toupées. The air smelled of mushroom soup. Cream of. He stayed focused on the door, which led to the foyer beyond, where the receptionist had welcomed him only minutes before.

Now it was stuck. He peered through the glass to catch the receptionist's eye. She was gone. *Shit*. Daniel cracked his knuckles, one at a time – a ten-step arpeggio – before trying again. But nothing. He was trapped. Twenty-one years old today and yet here he would remain, caged in with the dying, reading books and pruning bonsai trees and eating nothing but condensed bloody soup.

Then again, a tiny voice mused, *it could be good research*.

But he wouldn't let the joke stick. He didn't like his job; didn't like being an obiturist; didn't even like old people – yet another reason why he knew he shouldn't have come here in the first place. In fact, as soon as he'd opened that 21st Birthday card and read the half-familiar scrawls and the return address: 'Jewish Home of Ireland', he should have just chucked it away and made sure his father, and stepmother and half-brother never saw. Headed off to mass like any other Sunday. The silence had been working fine all these years, why change it now?

But instead, he said nothing, and came. Only to be met with more nothing.

Daniel coughed. He wished he could click his throat like the rest of him – click the guilt away. Because he hated keeping secrets from his father. They'd stayed strong together since his mother's death; since the day he was born. 'A real team, eh, Danny boy?' He supposed that was the reason he'd stopped seeing his Zayde ... his grandfather in the first place. The old man had always been so cold towards his former son-in-law. So bitter.

Daniel clicked his neck, left and then right.

And then Gráinne had come along, and so new grandparents (or step-at least), and then baby Donal – a stranger to Zayde entirely – and suddenly Daniel felt embarrassed of this quirky old man with his cartoon nickname and his skullcap and that strange mezuzah thing beside the door to his house – 'the house where your mother grew up' – *but she's dead now*, Daniel wanted to scream – *I killed her!*

These days, dead people were Daniel's living; examining their pasts, composing their narratives, start, middle and end. Because other people's lives he could do. Of course, there was always some pressure to it – these were the words by which people were remembered – all a life was reduced to, in the end. Although he wrote most of them while they were still alive. It felt almost ominous. Like the Jewish superstition of not making a will in case it tempts fate. Well, his mother certainly hadn't been tempted. His mother – his first paragraph – maybe even his opening sentence. But he should have just left it there, and ignored the urge to open it all up again just because of some stupid card. There was nothing more to say – his grandfather had proven that once and for all now – so why was he still standing here? Why wasn't he gone?

Daniel shut his eyes, tasting the frustration on his lips. Mushroom soup. Cream of. And then, slowly, he began to click.

First his fingers, then his toes, there in his oversized shoes. And then his wrists, his neck, his back, his hips and anywhere else he could possibly find, exhaling with each release. Pleasure-pain.

And then the latch clicked too.

Daniel opened his eyes. The receptionist smiled. The door swung back like a half-spread wing. Just watching it, breath held, Daniel felt freer already.

Until suddenly, he felt something else.

He looked down at the fingers around his wrist. He traced where the wrinkles led. He reached the eyes, overflowing with words that didn't need to be spoken.

The old man gave a gentle nod, never blinking once. And then, just like that, he melted.

Return

'It's me, Daniel ... Daniel Murphy. Your Daniel. Don't you remember?' he says.

Ah sure, of course I remember you, you gobshite! my mind replies.

Gobshite – my very favourite curse. Mamzer comes in a close second, though because it's Hebrew it should probably win on aggregate – playing away from home and all that. But a gob full of shite, sure, you can't beat that.

Maybe that's why I've gone quiet these days – just too full of shite to speak. Though I'd spit it all out if I could. 'Elective Mutism' the doctor calls it, the smug little mamzer, but I didn't 'elect' for things to turn out this way – democracy my arse! It was just … with the missus gone (may her name be blessed), and then my daughter (may hers too), and then my grandson (and I suppose his as well), and then my independence … well, I suppose my voice just followed suit.

And yet suddenly here he is, looming before me, about twice the bloody size as when I last saw him. Certainly twice the size of me now anyway. Us Jews aren't exactly the tallest lot, so I suppose his height only proves which side he ended up on.

Haven't seen him in years – since he was … thirteen? He used to come round once a month. I'd read him stories. Sometimes I'd give him a few to take home with him, but he'd go all tense and start all his knuckle-clicking malarkey – like jigsaw pieces slotting into place – so I didn't push it. Other times we'd go strolling along Sandymount Strand, where the tide always looks as if it's sucking its stomach in, and I'd tell him more tales of a faraway land, a Promised one; one that belonged to him too, if only he knew. And I watched as every word traced its way down his spine, slotting its pieces somewhere else entirely.

But by thirteen, I suppose, he just grew out of all that. Or at least, grew out of me. Maybe that's what's after happening to my voice now too.

'Well if you've nothing to say, never mind, so.'

The door slams. The books shiver. The one at the top of Pile 14 billows open and a scrap of paper bursts free, riding the gust to the ground.

Shite.

Because I'll have to clamber out of bed now and put it back in its place. Because everything must be 'just so'. 'OCD' Doctor Mamzer calls it – load of shite you ask me – O.bsessive C.ompulsive D.iarrhoea would be more like it! He claims it's linked to the 'disappearance' of my speech. Disappearance – do you hear him – as if I could just take out a missing person's ad: HAVE YOU SEEN THIS VOICE?

I shake my head and uncurl my legs. An audible creak. I hope that doesn't count? Usually the nurses help me, but it's too early yet – they know I like to stay in bed 'til noon. Though God knows why I bother getting up at all.

I hang my legs over the side of the bed as if over a boat, the lino floor my sea. My desk lamp the feeble lighthouse. It winks. And now I am back there again, at the edge of the Strand, staring out at the swell.

'We came from beyond there, you know?'

He cracks his wrist. Morse code for confusion.

'We're a wandering people, Daniel. But we'll go Home eventually. *Next year in Jerusalem*, as they say.'

'But ... but this is my home, Zayde.'

His tears are like diamonds. My most prized possession.

But no, enough of that, you old fart – that's in the past now – and this scrap has to be tidied up immediately. *Focus!* I heave myself upwards without a sound. Lot harder than you think. Sneezing's the worst – that sound that just bursts out of you as if it's been captive for eternity. Or at least, for thousands of years. And even when somebody else does it, I always used to bless them – in Hebrew or English or even sometimes in Irish – *Dia linn* – 'God be with us'. Though I've always found it greedy counting yourself in on someone else's sneeze.

I lower my feet to the floor – watch out for those bloody cracks – jellyfish that sting. I reach down for the paper.

John O'Reilly (may his name be blessed).

Never heard of him, poor mamzer. Never heard of any of these people whose lives I've cut out of the newspaper, pored over line by line, and placed inside every last book I own like flowers in a flower press, keeping them fresh. Paperback burials. But it's not them I care about – it's him. Because above all, these are his words.

Daniel Murphy (may his name be ...)

My eyes leap to the door. Hold on a second – did he just ... was that really ...

You MAMZER! You eejit! You absolute schmuck! That was him – that wasn't a memory – that was really him! So why didn't you say something? Do something? Anything? You giant bloody gobshite!

My favourite curse finally shuts me up; my mind as still as my tongue. Everything clicking.

The lino's bloody freezing as I go. My body stiff. I imagine I either look constipated or like I'm about to drop an entire hurling team of kids off at the pool as I waddle forth. Full of shite – I told you! But no one pays attention. Since they cannot hear me, I swear sometimes they don't even bother to see.

In the rec room they're watching *Antiques Roadshow. Just pile us all into a van, sure, and we'd be ready to go!* But no time for jokes, no, only jittering along the too-shiny floor – skidding atop the sea.

Until my grandson comes into sight.

I move to shuffle forwards – to catch the attention I only just rejected. But suddenly he is moving himself, violently. I stop where I smile.

First his fingers crack, bone out of socket, and then his toes and his ankles and all the rest, breaking free. He stretches out with each sound, as if it is the noise of him growing – a fast-forwarded replay of the eight years I missed – evolution apace. It is beautiful.

But then he seems to snap out of it, reaching for the door, and suddenly time is imminent again. So I waddle, quickly, but somehow he doesn't hear my toes, or my breath, or the thud of my heart. I want to call out. If he's come back then maybe I can – maybe the silence is finished at last – O.ver in C.ompany of D.aniel!

But at last, my fingertips find him. The wrist bone is surprisingly warm. And by the time he gives them to me, the eyes are filled with diamonds. It is beautiful.

Ruth Gilligan is from Dublin, Ireland and studied at Cambridge University and Yale University before coming to UEA. She has published three bestselling commercial novels to date, but is now working towards a more mature, literary style as she writes her new novel, based around the history of Irish Jews.

Anthony Good

No Punishment Without Law

An extract from a novel in progress

When Kendrick left the car it was just barely raining, more a wetness felt in the air than rain. There were sirens in the distance. He wished he'd brought his coat – he felt too exposed in his grey suit. It was before five pm, but already the streetlights tinted the roads orange. From the car the tower block had just one window lit up yellow; he wasn't sure whether it was Silvia's flat. He felt like Jack approaching the stem of the beanstalk. As he came closer to the entrance he was glad to see some other lighted windows, on different faces of the building. At the intercom he struggled to remember the number of Silvia's flat. He pressed five-seven before hesitating. The red LED display had an industrial quality, as if its buttons could do more than simply ring a handset in a flat. He pressed DIAL, and dreaded he had the wrong number. He winced in the rain and there was no answer – just a click as the door unlocked. Surprised, but relieved, he grabbed the metal handle and pulled it open.

He glanced at the caretaker's office ahead, but there was only a fleece draped over a chair and the dull noise of a television. Walking towards the lifts, he jumped as the door slammed shut behind him. The lift smelled faintly of urine. The doors stayed open uncomfortably long. There were loud voices somewhere above. Kendrick only hoped they were not on Silvia's floor, which he did remember: floor six.

Leaving the lift he could hear the voices, closer, but still somewhere up above – angry, and shouting, but laughing also, aggressive speech and spirited cackling. The hallway was empty. Kendrick noticed for the first time the grey steel barricades over some of the doors. He must have assumed they were some kind of security feature, like the barred gates that were installed on some of the flats; only now was it clear that these impenetrable grey barriers permanently stopped anyone going into the flat. Silvia had told him that the place was condemned. He tried to avoid discussing her home, in fact he avoided thinking about it at all if he could. So he only realised now that the next time anyone would go into these sealed flats would be to remove everything inside, including the windows and copper wiring. For a brief time the wind would breathe through the glassless tower. And then there would be nothing there but sky.

He recognised Silvia's door, making a mental note of the number this time, and knocked. The bell had been broken for years; since before Silvia and her mother lived there. As he waited for her, there was an eruption of laughter above. The echo seemed to linger in the hallway. Kendrick knocked again, louder. He began to worry that Silvia had forgotten about him and gone out somewhere, or left intentionally before he arrived.

A voice came through the door. 'Who is it?'

'Silvia, it's me, Ken.'

As she opened the door slowly she looked almost annoyed, 'You didn't buzz, was the door open?'

'Yeah.' As he walked in, he added, 'Some other people were coming in.'

Once inside the flat he felt safe, though he was always alert for the return of Silvia's mother.

'How was work?' she said, as he took off his jacket and draped it over the sofa. He gave an uncommitted shrug. He was going to ask how her day was, but didn't want to refer to school. Instead he sighed. He had developed a relationship with Silvia wherein he was overworked and unsatisfied, and in need of rejuvenating, in need of her youth, which she gladly provided. In his moments of honesty with himself, Kendrick couldn't say quite what he provided for her. He had assumed it was the glamour of sleeping with a television producer – but she didn't even want to be a TV presenter. Perhaps she enjoyed the idea he was married, and older, or maybe it was somehow convenient, to be sleeping with someone far out of her own social circle, mostly disconnected from her life. In truth that was what Kendrick enjoyed too.

'It can't be that bad.'

He struggled for something to say. The reality was far too bland. He couldn't admit that he'd simply left the office out of boredom, after making a few token, and pointless, telephone calls. As much as it spoke of the authority he held, it didn't quite maintain the illusion he wanted. 'I was in a meeting today, and it just confirmed that actors are arseholes.'

Silvia grinned. She enjoyed discussing actors and behind the scenes, especially treating these extraordinary things as bland or, even better, outright deriding them. She sat next to him. 'Was it anyone famous?'

Propelled by her question, he eased into the sofa and continued, 'No, that was the worst part, but they all think they're so important. Obviously he's convinced he's the next Brando – '

'What was he being a dick about?'

He took his time picking a topic for his character's disdain. He inhaled her curiosity. 'The script, like always. Wanted to change it – to enlarge his part obviously. Add a few scenes, stuff like that.'

'What an arse.'

He was pleased by how willingly she took his side. His wife would do the same, but she didn't have the same attentiveness. She tended to accept his stories with bored compliance, even when they were true.

'But that's TV. That's just the way the industry is. It's an industry of arseholes.' He smiled at his own aloofness. Then the nagging dread of Silvia's mother resurfaced in Kendrick's mind. 'How's your mum?'

She frowned comically at the implied connection between the two thoughts. 'She's fine.' Sensing that wasn't the information he was after, she continued, 'She's on a double shift today. So she's got tomorrow off.'

His relief was visible as he relaxed into the sofa. Silvia smiled at him. 'D'you want a drink?'

Kendrick gave a sideways nod. 'That'd be great.' Silvia bounced off the sofa and went into the kitchen. Kendrick looked at her buttocks as she was gazing into the fridge.

'Is a beer all right?'

Still looking at her buttocks he said, 'A beer would be nice, thanks.'

She turned with a blue tin in each hand, elbowing the fridge door shut. They smiled at each other, Kendrick eyeing her as she walked back to the sofa, the fabric of her trousers gripping her thighs. She sat down, and immediately he was aroused by her proximity. She handed him a tin, and they cracked them open, Kendrick taking a nervous sip.

As he jogged down the stairwell he observed the details of the tower's disrepair, rejoicing to be leaving. On the fifth floor the wall panelling below the window had shoeprints, as if someone had tried to kick it out entirely. For what reason Kendrick couldn't imagine. Further down, a window had a large radial crack, roughly head height. He dodged past dubious wet patches before a loud shout slowed his pace. He nearly stopped completely, before there was another noise, a murmur, and then loud laughter again.

Just below him a group of black boys entered the stairwell, laughing and shouting. Kendrick was caught at the top of the flight of stairs overlooking them – no way to disappear, no way to turn and walk away without causing offence, or drawing attention. He nearly froze as one of the boys looked at him, and looked at his clothes and shoes. He continued down the steps slowly, trying to seem casual, and unconcerned. Another of the boys glanced at him, before all three of them began walking down, speaking loudly with sudden exclamations.

'He got jooked up, boy! He got jooked up!'

Kendrick slowed almost entirely, waiting to give them a sufficient head start, just in case they changed their minds and came back for him. His heart was beating loud in his head. When he could hear that the boys had gone he continued down the stairs, elated by the hormonal surge, his fingers shaking and light. He nearly laughed to himself at his foolish paranoia, taking each step slowly to the bottom.

Outside the sky was now completely dark. It was nearly eight. His phone told him he had missed three calls from his wife. He started constructing the bare bones of his alibi as he made his way to the car, still invigorated by his close encounter with danger in the stairwell. The slow rain had stopped. The ground was slick. He decided on a simple lie: he would transpose his meeting yesterday afternoon to this evening. It saved on having to create the smaller details, and fundamentally reduced the extent of his lie. As he got near his car he went over the conversation in his head, in preparation for his wife's curiosity. Kendrick's return home was often late, and he never knew what it was that prompted his wife to question him on some nights and not others.

He aimed the remote key at the car, but the single flash and hoot indicated the doors were now locked. As he was cursing himself for forgetting to lock the car he noticed a face. His stomach tightened as he recognised it was one of the black boys from before. There were two of them, across the road. The one closer by looked at him, the other seemed less interested. There was a manic intensity to his gaze, though Kendrick couldn't see him clearly under the orange light. Maybe it was the car's chirrup that had caught his attention. Kendrick pressed on the key again, and the car gave a double flash and cry to attract further scrutiny. He fumbled with the door handle, made unresponsive by his nerves, finally managing to pull open the door. The boy looked away and said something to his friend, who kicked a plastic bottle aggressively across the road. It bounced and hit the rear bumper of the car. As Kendrick started the engine he glanced at the boys, in case they should make their way over to him. One of them looked at him as he pulled away. He kept his eyes on the road and concentrated on driving safely away. As he put the boys behind him and reached the end of the road he heard one of them yell loudly, 'Joker!'

Turning onto the High Street, he felt sheltered by the other cars, and pedestrians, but a certain dread lingered in his mind. He turned on the radio to distract him from his nerves. Though he wasn't listening, the sound of the DJ's voice soothed him. He began to feel the relief of escape for the second time that night. But he couldn't escape the feeling of danger. Perhaps it was just a heightened state of awareness, the awareness of how thinly he was protected from the outside. The street felt close. Maybe this was his dread. He tried to distract himself by thinking of what he'd say to his wife when he got home. As the traffic crawled forward he ran through a menu of questions, to proof his alibi for cracks. He reminded himself of the conversation he'd had with another producer, trying to remember one of the jokes he'd laughed at, if there'd been one.

He slowed at a traffic light, and seemed to sense the terrible realisation before it happened, as if his subconscious had suppressed the awful and bizarre truth up until this moment. Maybe he had noticed, but somehow not registered, the shape in the backseat when he got into the car. First it was the voice.

'Don't fucking stop driving.'

Kendrick nearly gagged. The boy's face seemed to rise up from nowhere in the rear-view mirror. The car jolted to a stop.

'Don't fucking stop driving!'

Shaking, he pushed down on the accelerator, bouncing the car forward, nearly colliding with the car ahead.

'Don't fucking stop!'

Anthony Good was born in Brussels in 1986, and grew up in Portugal and England. He studied English at University College, Oxford, and was awarded the UEA Booker Scholarship 2010-11. He is currently working on a novel about a detective, a firearms officer and a television executive.

Hannah Harper

The Terrible Testimony of Cordelia Scar

I was born on a frosty night in late November, and my parents, Angus and Teresa Scar, took the liberty of giving their baby daughter two rather unusual middle names as well as a first which was intimidating in both stature and connotation; so that the name finally printed on the birth certificate I held for a while before burning, twenty-nine years later, read: Cordelia – Edgware – Paddington – Scar. Cordelia, because they felt certain that a 'woman of rare honesty' already lurked behind my solemn eyes; and also because, as my mother reasoned, they could shorten it to 'Lia' without too much trouble, and it would still sound 'feminine.'

'One letter short of liar, you know,' was all my father said about that. He was a silent man, a Christian-turned-atheist after the simultaneous deaths of his sister and brother-in-law two years prior to my birth, though the conversion was not for the reason you might think. Far from railing against God for taking the pair too soon, his despair and disbelief was because they'd left their two-year-old daughter, Annie, to his and Teresa's care. My parents did not want a child then, although in their own way, they did their best to embrace Annie as their own. But she was a troubled, difficult personality, and remained so for as long as she was with us. She never liked me, either. I cannot stand not being liked.

At the age of sixteen I made my first abortive attempt at writing my memoirs. On the subject of my middle names, I wrote this:

My two middle names are Edgware and Paddington; the first because it's where I was born at, and the second because it's where my mother and father were travelling to at the time. I think this is entirely ridiculous. My mother, I suspect, thinks it's rather cosmopolitan. They also like to boast that I am a 'tube baby' – and when people ask about it, presuming they mean 'test tube', they love it, and correct them, explaining they mean 'tube' as in 'London Underground' tube, as further evidence of their cosmopolitan ways. I have never been impressed; neither, as far as I'm aware, has anyone else. I suppose I should be grateful they left the 'Road' out.

On the fact of my birth, however, I remain impressed by my wisdom and acuity concerning my family situation. I'd arrived at the conclusion that:

'To make him stay, my mother had me. It wasn't like when failing couples have a baby in a pointless effort to seal the cracks. No. When it happened – I happened – I think they were 'in love' and had been together for a while – and he hoped for children and she didn't – and she wanted to make him happy. So after a long time she got pregnant, and in the end I think she ended up loving me more than he did.'

It was a love I could not return. I couldn't bear it when she picked me up from school – luckily, she did not make a habit of this – and she would smile at the school gates, hoping I'd run to her like all the other little girls ran to their mothers. But I did not want her to be there. I did not want her to see how unpopular I was; yes, that was a part of it. But also, I didn't want to see how she was whispered about. Little ripples of whispers, reeds in the breeze, *that's Lia's mum,* and then the theatrical hand pressed down hard on a rising smirk – all aimed at my mother, with her fleshy bulk and her big mole on her chin, her lank, spidery hair and her unusual voice, horsey and wheezing and so indiscreet. I could not, even as a small child, feign unawareness of the indiscreet. It offended me then as it does so now.

The four of us – my silent, truculent father, my fat, apologetic mother, my unstable, taciturn cousin, and me – lived in a large and draughty house called Number 1, The Eaves. 'The Eaves' was too grand a name for the groaning, ancient monstrosity it was, with its peeling windows prone to sweaty condensation in the winter months and wanton forest of a back garden. There had evidently been an attempt at a patio just outside the back door, where forlorn gnomes huddled together as though planning an already doomed coup.

The various furniture left behind by a parade of former inhabitants contributed to the haphazard, absent-minded quality that prevailed in the Eaves. It used to be a student house, and I found some ancient scribbles in silvery pencil on the side of the high bunk I slept on until I was twelve. 'On this bed, my penis entered a girl' was one of the phrases I read. It didn't make any kind of impression on me then. When I was old enough to know more about the machinations of sex, though, I imagined an etiolated male, banging his buttocks on the ceiling in a frenzy of sheets and desire, while a pale-limbed girl writhed under him in showy ecstasy.

In our dining room, an ornate, thick red rug was flung over the bare floorboards to cover the splinters and stray nails there. My parents didn't believe in 'mollycoddling' us children with anything as pedestrian as a properly-fitted carpet. There was a tall lamp with a brown tasselled shade, and a heavy, gilded mirror propped against the wall next to it. When I was very young, I used to stand in front of its dusty surface and play blinking games with myself. As I got a bit older – six, perhaps, or seven – I'd stare and stare at myself, until I became quite a stranger to my own features. There was a stillness about my face, I decided, and something about my black hair and sullen mouth that was perhaps the reason why the other children at school kept well away from me, and were mean whenever they were forced to interact with me by some well-intentioned teacher or assistant on playground duty. I liked to watch my reflection as twilight sifted into the room. I would end up sitting in darkness, and fancy that my eyes gleamed like crocodiles submerged in oily depths. Once, I kissed myself. I leaned forward and touched my mouth to the mirror mouth. Then I felt guilty, and quickly wiped the glass with my sleeve and left the room.

Cousin Annie used to enrage me by calling me 'the strange little child', even though she was hardly more normal, with her arms mottled blue and her scabbed neck she used to pick incessantly with nervous fingers. But I could never make my retorts hurt her. I wanted my words to rain like nails into her skin, I wanted them to draw blood, I hated her so much. But she always behaved like she'd never heard me. One day, she was taunting me about my habit of talking to myself, and I called her a 'parent-stealer.' No sooner had the words flown out of my mouth than I felt a thrilling tingling in the air before my lips, a dangerous thrumming, and I almost laughed in excitement to see what she'd do next. But she would never behave how you expected her to, and on that occasion she said nothing and simply left the room. Drifted out of the room, rather, with none of the forced nonchalance you might expect from someone who has just borne a fair jibe from a now-equal enemy and has gone to lick their wounds.

Annie would stay in her room for days, not responding to pleas, cajoling or knocks from my parents and rarely eating the food left on a tray outside her door. I knew my parents thought it was because of traumatic memories of her parents and the car crash that took them; Annie was the sole survivor, pink-faced and screaming in the back seat as her parents were cut out of the front. But really, I wasn't sure what was wrong with her; only that something was, and it made her difficult to live with.

When I was ten, and Annie fourteen, she drank bleach in front of me. She intended to kill herself, and she achieved it; so that, perhaps, was something. However, for me it was an unpleasant episode.

I remember it clearly. A Saturday afternoon, and I was playing by myself; that meant I was moodily snipping up the bottom of the curtains in the dining room to create a fringed effect that I knew would earn me a smack later on. Snip, snip, snip; the material was heavy and grey, but I'd taken the best kitchen scissors, the ones used to trim flower stems and slice through meat packages, and they were making light work of the tough, veiny weave. I felt satisfied.

Annie came downstairs. In fact, as I observed without interest, she was weaving slowly, the way a rabid dog does before its jaws go rigid and its mouth starts to foam. She came to a stop in the doorway and looked at me, but her eyes were unfocused. She was holding an oversized mug in her hand.

'Good morning,' I said, pleasantly but warily.

'Except that it's not,' Annie said. 'I'm sick of it, Lia.'

That in itself was unusual; she called me 'Lia', not 'weirdo', not 'strange child', not 'pixie witch', which was a new one she'd adopted recently. She was wearing a blue dressing gown and the same pair of pyjamas she'd been wearing for weeks. Then she started to bang her forehead against the doorframe.

I was still unimpressed. I'd seen this routine before. My parents usually ignored her when she did it in front of them and so I followed suit. She rarely hit hard enough to draw blood, although once she did knock herself out. That earned her a lengthy doctor's appointment with Dr. Palmer, and when Annie and my mother came home that evening my mother was quivering with the necessary silence of it all.

As she banged, I snipped faster on the curtain. Blue liquid slopped out of the mug and over her hand. This did interest me. I don't know if I registered then that it was bleach, but feeling it on her hand seemed to remind Annie it was there, and then, without looking at me, she gulped the entire contents of the mug down. Then it fell from her hand onto the floorboards but didn't break. It rolled.

She fell forward into an oblong of sunlight, and a long splinter sank deep into her knee. But she didn't seem to notice, and she was making a dreadful noise – *ungagh, ungagh, ungagh* – rather like a retch, but nothing came up. I read up on it later, and I discovered that this would have been caused by the bleach eating through her tongue and burning the soft tissue in her mouth, dissolving her gums and destroying her throat. She looked at me, but there was no appeal in her eyes.

Then the retching worked. Thin trails of blood and bile crept from her slack mouth, where they hung; she tried to spit them free but her energy was waning. In effect, I watched her die, and it never once occurred to me to call for either of my parents. It felt like fate was taking place, and it was not up to me to interfere. But when, later in the hospital, the doctor shook his head and said words like 'industrial strength' and 'cell death', and my mother shook me by the shoulders, over and over again, and kept asking, 'why didn't you call us, why didn't you call us, why, why, why' – my reasoning seemed insufficient. It was the truth; but I think they would have thought it an insult. So I kept quiet.

Hannah Harper was born in Reading in 1983 and studied literature at the University of Sheffield, where she read for both undergraduate and postgraduate degrees. She has worked as a receptionist, copywriter, and bookseller and is currently completing her first novel.

Emma Healey

Novel Extract

This is an extract from a novel about an elderly Alzheimer's sufferer – Maud – who is convinced that her friend Elizabeth has gone missing. Dismissed as forgetful, Maud is determined to investigate anyway, spurred on by the memory of her sister's disappearance in the 1940s.

I don't know where we are. I can see it's a restaurant – waiters in black and white, marble-topped tables – but which one? I have an awful feeling I'm supposed to know and that this is some kind of treat. I don't think it's my birthday. Perhaps it's an anniversary. Patrick's death? It would be just like Helen to remember and make it a 'special occasion'. But it's winter and Patrick died in the spring, so it can't be that. The menu says *The Olive Grill*. It's heavy, the cover leathery. I can't keep it upright; the end of the spine slips on the tabletop. I pull it onto my lap and read it aloud: 'Butternut squash soup. Tomato and mozzarella salad. Garlic mushrooms. Parma ham and melon—'

'Yep, thanks Mum,' Helen says. 'I can read the menu myself.'

My daughter doesn't like me reading things out. She always sighs and rolls her eyes. Sometimes she makes gestures behind my back. I've seen her in mirrors pretending to strangle me. She lowers her menu now, but keeps her eyes on it.

'What are you going to have? You usually like soup.'

'I have soup at Elizabeth's sometimes,' I say, a thought coming to me. I still haven't heard from Elizabeth. Not a word. I can't understand it; she never goes away. Something must have happened. 'Elizabeth is missing.

Did I tell you?' I am looking at Helen, but she isn't looking at me.

'You said. What are you going to eat?'

I sit staring over the top of my menu. The restaurant is a blur of colours. The walls are red and blue streaked, and the side plates are black. I suppose that must be fashionable. One of the walls seems just to be glass; it makes me nervous.

'Mum? You've got to order.'

A waiter comes and stands by our table, notepad out ready. He bends right over to ask us what we want, his face unnecessarily close to mine. I lean away from him. 'Helen, you haven't heard anything about Elizabeth, have you?' I say. 'You would tell me if you had?'

'Yes, Mum. What are you going to eat?'

'It's not like she can go off on holiday,' I say, closing the menu and looking for somewhere to rest it. I can't find a space. There are too many things on the table. Shiny things. I can't think what they are.

'Something must have happened to her. If she'd had a fall I wouldn't know you see. I doubt her son would bother to tell me.'

The waiter straightens up and takes the menu from my hands. Helen smiles at him and orders for us both – I don't know what. He nods and wanders off, still writing.

'This is the problem,' I say, not wanting to forget my subject. '*Families* are informed but not friends. Not at our age anyway.'

'This used to be a Chophouse, d'you remember, Mum?' Helen breaks in.

What was I saying? I can't remember. Something. Something something something ...

'Do you remember?'

I'm blank.

'You used to meet Dad here, didn't you?'

I look around the room. There are two old women at a table by a blue-streaked wall. 'Elizabeth is missing,' I say.

'When it was a Chophouse. For tea.'

'Her phone rings and rings ... '

'A Chophouse. Remember? Oh, never mind.'

Helen sighs again. She's doing a lot of that lately. She won't listen, won't take me seriously. Imagines that I want to live in the past. I know what she's thinking – that I've lost my marbles. That Elizabeth is perfectly well at home and I just don't remember having seen her recently. But it's not true. I forget things – I know that – but I'm not mad. Not yet. And I'm sick of being treated as if I am. I'm tired of the sympathetic smiles and the little pats people give you when you get things confused, and I'm bloody fed up with everyone deferring to Helen rather than listening to what I have to say.

My heartbeat quickens and I clench my teeth. I have a terrible urge to kick Helen under the table. I kick the table leg instead. The shiny salt and pepper shakers rattle against each other and a wine glass starts to topple. Helen catches it.

'Mum,' she says. 'Be careful. You'll break something.'

I don't answer; my teeth are still tight together. I feel I might start screaming. But breaking something. That's a good idea. That's exactly what I want to do. I pick up my butter knife and stab it into my plate. The china breaks. Helen says something. Swearing I think. And somebody rushes towards me. I keep looking at the plate. The middle has crumbled slightly. It looks like a broken record. A broken gramophone record. I found some once in our back garden.

They were in the vegetable patch, smashed to bits and all jumbled together. Ma had sent me out to help Dad when I'd got back from school. He was at the end of the garden, digging a trench for runner beans and I was sowing radish seeds. The records were almost the same colour as the soil and I wouldn't have found them, only the shards got caught between the prongs of my garden fork.

When I realised what they were I scraped all the bits out of the earth and dropped them into a sunny patch of grass to dry. Then I brushed the dirt off and began to fit them back together, not because I thought they'd play, just to see which ones they were. I couldn't think where they'd come from; only Douglas, our lodger, had a gramophone and I thought he'd have said if any of his records had broken, and he wasn't the sort to dump things in the garden anyway.

Ma came out to collect some washing and found me kneeling over the pieces.

'What on earth are they?' she asked.

When I told her she said she thought it must be the neighbours who'd chucked them over the fence.

'I'll have a word with them,' she said. 'It's not the first time I've found their rubbish out here.' She looked down at the records. 'Fancy breaking all these. Good for nothing now. Hey, Maud, put them in the bottom of the runner bean trench. For drainage.'

'All right,' I said. 'I just want to put them together first.'

'Why? You making stepping stones for the lawn?'

'Could I?'

'Don't be daft.'

She laughed and stepped daintily from one broken bit to another, the washing basket on her hip, until she was at the kitchen door.

It didn't take me long to connect all the pieces, and it was nice work in the sun; just like doing a jigsaw puzzle, except that even when I'd finished there were still some bits missing. I could read the labels now though: *Virginia, Cruel is He* and *I'm Nobody's Baby*. I sat back on my heels. They were all my sister's favourites, the ones she often asked Douglas to play. And now here they were, smashed up and buried amongst the rhubarb and onions. I couldn't think who would do it or why. I shuffled the bits together again and took them to Dad, scattering them into the trench. When I walked back to the house I saw Douglas standing at his window staring down at me.

I can't think now whether that was before or after my sister disappeared.

I'm finishing an ice cream. It's nice and cold against my tongue, but I can't work out what flavour it's meant to be. Strawberry, I suppose, from the colour.

Helen is getting her coat on. 'I have to pick Katy up in less than half an hour,' she says.

I need the loo. I wonder where the ladies' is. I wonder if I've been to this restaurant before. It reminds me of the lovely old Chophouse that Patrick and I used to meet in. It wasn't expensive, didn't have exotic food or white tablecloths, but everything was nicely cooked and well laid out. I used to wait at a table by the window and Patrick would come loping along, hair swept about and cheeks red, and he'd grin as soon as he saw me. No one grins at me like that now.

'Do you need the loo, Mum?' Helen's holding my coat out for me.

'Haven't I been?'

'Have you? OK then,' she shrugs. 'Let's go.'

She's not very pleased with me. I've obviously done something. Was it embarrassing? Did I say something to the waiter? I don't like to ask. I told a woman once that her teeth made her look like a horse. I remember Helen telling me I'd said it, but I don't remember saying it.

'Are we going home?' I ask instead.

'Yes, Mum.'

In the car I look out of the window. The sun went down while we were eating and the sky is an inky colour. I can still see the road signs though, and am reading them aloud before I know it: 'Give Way. Level Crossing. Reduce your speed.' Helen's hands go white on the steering wheel. She doesn't speak to me. I shift in my seat, suddenly aware of my full bladder.

'Are we going home?'

Helen sighs. This means I've asked before. As we turn onto my street I realise how urgent my need to go is. I can't sit any longer.

'Drop me here,' I say to Helen, scrabbling at the door handle.

'Don't be silly, we're nearly there now,' she says.

I open the door anyway. Helen stops the car with a jerk.

'What the hell d'you think you're doing?' she says.

I scramble out of the car and make off down the road.

'Mum?' Helen calls, but I don't turn round.

I hurry towards my door, body bent forward. Every few seconds an extra hard squeeze of the muscles is required. The pressure in my bladder seems greater the closer I come to home. I unbutton my coat as I walk and grope desperately for my key. At the door I shift from foot to foot, frantically twisting the key in the lock. Something is stopping it from turning properly.

'Oh no oh no,' I moan aloud.

Finally I feel it catch and turn. I fall through the door and slam it behind me, handbag thudding to the floor. Clawing at the banister, I rush up the stairs, coat sailing down to the bottom as I shrug it off. I get to the bathroom. But it's too late; hand on my waistband, I begin to wee.

I tear down my trousers, but have no time for the rest, and so sit on the loo urinating through my cotton knickers. For a few moments I let myself slump forward, head on hands, elbows on knees, the sodden trousers clinging round my ankles. Then slowly and awkwardly I kick off my shoes and pull the thick wet fabric over my feet, dropping it into the bath.

There are no lights on in the house – I'd no time to switch any on – and so I sit in the dark. And begin to cry.

Emma Healey was born and grew up in London where she worked in the art world after completing her first degree in bookbinding – during which she learned how to put books together, but not how to write them. She is now finishing her first novel.

Debra Isaac

Dina

The following is an extract from a short story describing a fictional meeting between the narrator and Dina Vierny, the muse of the French sculptor Aristide Maillol. Vierny died, aged 89, in 2009.

It was the young man working at the front desk who told me she was coming.

When I first came to the museum on Tuesday, he wasn't particularly helpful. He sold me a ticket and seemed keen to limit my questions. You would have thought he was working at the Grand Palais with a queue of people impatient to get in.

But few people come here. It's rather out of the way and besides, the holiday season is over. You see young people standing on the road next to trucks and vast plastic bins filled with grapes. There are posters in town for a festival marking the end of the harvest.

When I returned the following day, he greeted me more warmly but seemed surprised to see me.

Hello again. What brings you back?

Perhaps few people ever visit this museum twice. It is a small museum.

He looks young enough to be at university. He even smells like a student. I don't think he brushes his hair, or perhaps he deliberately musses it up. Each time I've seen him, he's worn the same Warhol T-shirt – *Art is what you can get away with*, imprinted on the face of the *Mona Lisa* – and beads around his neck.

Are you especially interested in Maillol? he asked.

I told him it was Dina who interested me.

Would I still be here on Friday?

You're in luck, he said. She's coming here on Friday.

This really is too much, isn't it? That Dina should turn up in Banyuls just when I'm visiting? Isn't it strange how one thing has led to another? If I hadn't read your book, we wouldn't have talked about Dina. If you and I hadn't met, I would never have thought of visiting the museum. If Charles and I hadn't broken up, I wouldn't have been free to come here.

The young man, whose name is Luc, says Dina hasn't been back in two years. Apparently, a member of Maillol's family met her in Perpignan this morning and has brought her to Banyuls. I'd like to talk to the man but Luc says he never speaks to strangers about Maillol. On the other hand, he may drive Dina to the museum so I may meet him anyway.

On Wednesday, I spent the entire morning at the museum. No one else was there – except Luc, of course. I could hardly miss the sculpture of *Harmony*; it stands alone in the first room.

You are right, it is one of Maillol's best. The bodies of his women are all so similar – the nymphet breasts and melon hips – but I liked Dina's inward expression in this one. The sculpture has a quietness, a meditative feel, perhaps because it was created here in these tranquil surroundings.

You would be furious, though, at the way they've done the lighting. It's far too harsh and scars the surface (bronze, unlike marble, doesn't eat electric light). There's no need for it either. With the windows wide open, there's plenty of natural light.

The museum closes between noon and four. Luc asked where I had parked my car. When I told him I'd walked here, he looked at me as if I was insane.

I said, Dina used to do it.

She had no choice, he said.

He offered to order a taxi from Banyuls. Or, if you really want to walk, he said, I could drop you at the main road.

I told him I would like to stay for a while, to sit in the shade of a tree and read.

Be my guest, he said, kindly, a little mocking. As you see, there are plenty of trees to choose from. Before he left, he came out to find me and gave me a bottle of cold water.

He has a motorbike, one of those flashing, powerful ones that wouldn't look out of place at midnight outside the Hôtel Costes. The engine rattles the earth. Birds' wings beat in the leaves when he starts it and the roots of the trees tremble. Everything waits.

After, when the noise has completely faded, the museum reverts to being a museum and the garden to being a garden.

If you sit on the grass for long enough, something else happens. The museum once again becomes a house where an artist-hermit spent his days, working, thinking, sleeping and eating simple food.

A figure in a beret stands on the steps, still as a church saint, his features carved in pine scented wood.

A girl with a knowing look appears on the path that runs beside the dried-out riverbed. Her skin is dark from the sun and she wears a chequered summer dress.

Watching from the shade of the cypress, you realise that one thing, at least, hasn't changed. Then, as now, Dina's visits were not ordinary events.

*

Luc suggested, tactfully, that perhaps it would be better if initially I stayed upstairs when Dina arrived. I'm sure he was told to say this by his cousin, Marie, who works part-time at the museum and is with him here today.

She is at least ten years older than Luc, reminiscent of those graceless curators you sometimes find with the mentality of prison wardens. She has a point though. The museum doesn't officially open until later and it would look odd to have an unknown woman waiting at the entrance ready to pounce on Dina the moment she appears.

It's rather arrogant anyway to expect to meet her, although I know what you'd say: don't worry, make the most of the opportunity. How I wish I had your ease and self-confidence.

I remind myself that Dina never had any qualms about introducing herself to people such as Gide even before she became a public figure. Perhaps she will understand – and it's not as if there's no connection between us, although just now it seems somewhat tenuous.

Marie unnerved me, though. I came here early and was sitting in the garden when she arrived with Luc. He and I have got to know each other a little and today he was immediately friendly, inviting me to wait inside the museum. He introduced me and had obviously told Marie something about why I am here. But I could see she was unhappy with the situation, possibly angry with him for telling a tourist about Dina's visit.

The museum re-opens at four, she said, and I thought she might bar my entry. Luc stepped back, into the shadow of the porch.

You propose an interview with Madame Vierny? Marie demanded, as if obtaining an interview might be a long process necessitating a formal request.

It's not so much an interview, I explained, more of a coincidence.

Your grandfather knew her? she asked, making it sound like an accusation.

Even when I confirmed that my grandfather knew Dina, she seemed unimpressed, as if anybody might be in a similar position, as if this in itself conveyed no privilege. She went inside without asking anything further.

Have I got you into trouble? I asked Luc. Should I forget the meeting? I told him I was happy to go away, or remain in the garden.

Neither of us knew what to do but for some reason Marie returned and invited me to go inside. I followed Luc and he suggested that I come up here. He led the way, apologising about Marie, explaining that Dina had just called and asked her to find certain documents by the time she arrives, on top of the ones Marie has already dug out.

I've been here for more than an hour now, upstairs by the window. Sometimes a bird delves into the dark leaves of a tree and I hear a breaking twig. White butterflies cartwheel on and off the windowsill. The scents of the garden pour into the room.

Sometimes the silence interrupts my flow of words, inviting me to look up, to discern which object is insisting on my attention. And I see a drawing of Dina, a young woman asleep in the sunlight, naked except for a slip of drapery that falls across her thigh.

There is mischief there, giving the lie to Dina's denial of anything improper between her and Maillol. Nevertheless, I believe what she said is true. There is mischief but also playfulness and trust; a sense of love in observation.

I feel instinctively that Maillol did the drawing here, on an afternoon such as this, soft charcoal lines blended from the earth and peace that surround the house. He is working over there, in the shade of the cedar, his sense of Dina almost complete on the paper, when she wakes beneath the embrace of the branches, pretending that she hasn't slept at all, that she closed her eyes only to create for him a deeper impression of repose.

He laughs, tells her she should go to bed earlier, and yet doesn't dismiss her words for it is Dina who has chosen where to lie down, where to position her arms, and where to drape the fragment of linen that he has brought with him from the house. He has recorded the shape of her; she has chosen who she will be.

But now I hear tyres on the gravel, voices and opening doors. Suddenly I feel nervous and wish that you were here to give me courage. Like you, I am never happier than when I'm alone in a gallery or museum but how do you behave when the real thing appears, when the *Venus de Milo* pulls up in her car?

Debra Isaac was born in London and studied Philosophy, Politics and Economics at Oxford. She has worked as a journalist and is currently writing a novel.

Jenny Karlsson

One: Noah
The first chapter of a novel

Noah wishes he could pick Lucy up, carry her away from the sink and the dishes into the other room and tie her to the armchair, just one hand free to use the remote control.

'I can do it,' he says for the second time. 'It goes with doing the cooking, you said so yourself.'

Lucy has the sleeves of her shell suit rolled up above her elbows as she rubs grease off the frying pan. Noah stands next to her by the sink, his shirt sleeves rolled up too. From over her shoulder, he looks at her hands: the scruffy scouring sponge and strong washing-up liquid are making them more red and wrinkly than they already were. Lucy turns on the tap and rotates the pan methodically beneath it so water splashes onto her apron. She gives Noah a look; he steps quietly to the side; she reaches past him and lays the pan on the dish rack.

'Fine,' Noah says eventually and leaves the kitchen, rolling down his sleeves.

He moves a magazine from a dining chair and sits down. He kicks off his slippers, jerks his foot as one slipper remains dangling on his toes. Using his feet, he sweeps his shoes towards him and bends down. His fingertips are a sickly white, thick and callused from assembling a million plastic components and coiling a million metal springs on the conveyor belts. On each shoe he ties a neat double bow.

'I'm going out,' he bellows in his factory hall voice.

Lucy appears in the doorway.

'Where on earth are you going?' She wipes her hands on a dishcloth, takes Noah in from the bows on his shoes to the buttons on the cuffs of his denim jacket. Her back is regally straight, her face soft, silky lines and her sky eyes sharp like little spikes.

'Might as well go and do the numbers.'

Noah licks the corner of his mouth, suppresses his smile – he remembered lottery day before Lucy did. Now she can have the dishes while he goes out. Her annoyance appears as a minimal rearrangement of the silken lines around her mouth. She gives almost nothing away.

'In that?' she says finally and nods at his unbuttoned jacket. He looks down at it. 'It's no warmer than the Arctic out there. You better put on your overcoat unless you fancy being a snowman.' He keeps suppressing his smile, she keeps wiping her red hands on the dishcloth, although they must be dry by now.

Noah hesitates before he wriggles out of the denim jacket and replaces it on its hook beside the door. He slides his big arms into the duffel coat and buttons it up. His smile spreads out, creasing the skin around his eyes. Lucy purses her lips, then she gently slaps him on the stomach with the dishcloth.

'Bye then,' Noah says. He waves a hand in the air as he leaves but Lucy has already turned on the tap again, water splattering testily against the metal sink.

~

After the dusky stairwell, the brightness outside is always blinding, regardless of the weather. Today there is a pale milky glow behind the clouds, the first trace of sun this year, its sheen making the metal doorframe glint like ice. In summer the door's steel handle is too hot to touch.

By the next door, a boy is balancing on a bicycle. Another boy watches, holding a piece of wood. Both waver silently there, like saplings. They stare at Noah, who says nothing to them; he squints up at the sky and walks along the path to the shops.

~

It's not that he wanted to wash the dishes. He just doesn't like the feeling of sitting, idling by, while Lucy busies herself. After he'd retired, he discovered that the running of their home was a secret, one Lucy intended to keep.

Today he cooked lunch – she let him do as much – but she kept appearing, remarking what a mess he was making, moving things. He tried to make her go and sit in the other room, said he'd clean everything up when he was done. She enjoyed the omelette he made; she likes his omelettes, she said. But she's running out of patience with him. She's running out of patience with a lot of things: the cold weather, the re-runs, the neighbours moving out, the neighbours moving in, and the rest. Maybe there's nothing he can do about it. Maybe there's something.

A row of modern lampposts stand on Noah's right, beyond them a row of houses, some hospitable, some not. He passes slowly. On his left, football fields stretch out, brown, almost grassless. At the end of the fields some trees poke the sky.

The air feels soft and sharp at the same time, like feathers and twigs on his cheeks. Aside from the wind, it is as if Noah is the only thing moving, the only thing visibly alive. Everything else is still or absent: no birds, no traffic, no people. He looks back, but the two boys have also disappeared. Only the fields tear up the low sky. Noah walks with his hands in his pockets, happy about the warm coat.

~

He stands by the counter at the far end of the shop, behind the broad backs of two other men who are filling in their tickets, filling up the space.

The shelves beside him are filled with sweets and chocolates and mints in colours that make him dizzy if he looks directly at them. But on the corner of the top shelf stands two perfectly straight, untouched rows of shiny chocolate rabbits. They are wrapped in gold-coloured foil that sort of crumbles when you peel it off. Noah picks one up and turns it over in his hand. A little bell jingles dully around its neck. He watches the rabbit sit on his palm with its outlined eyes wide open at the sides of its head. He folds his hand around it, careful not to break it, feeling the air inside the hollow inside the rabbit: air about the size of a heart.

One of the broad backs moves over to the queue at the counter and Noah takes his place at the lottery stand. The rabbit sits on the stand, watching as Noah draws black lines across the pink slip. The numbers are always the same: 1-5, Andrew's birthday; 17-7, Julia's birthday; 13-11, Ashleigh's birthday; and 26, meaning June second, Noah and Lucy's wedding day. A television screen above the stand gently pulsates big blue digits: seven million pounds, seven million pounds.

The boy behind the till takes the pink slip with his long fingers and hands Noah the ticket without looking at him, without saying a word. Afterwards Noah stands outside the newsagent, next to the woman who was before him in the queue. The woman stands holding a bag of doughnuts, turning her head this way then that, looking confused, as if she'd been readily assembled and spewed out from a factory without advice or warning.

A girl walks out of the chemist's next door to the newsagent's. She brushes Noah's arm. For half a second their eyes meet. Noah stares at her silently and she says sorry. He blinks and then he's sure: the girl is Little Abby, Little Abby who used to live next door, who Julia used to babysit. Her little round face and little uppity nose sitting right in the middle of it are just the same, but she is all grown up now, all glossy hair, high boots, and some sort of fluffy animal hanging around her neck. Abby shows no recognition as she turns and walks away beside the low grey wall to where a couple of cars are parked. By a shiny blue car, Abby meets a man in a suit. Their heads connect briefly in a kiss. The man looks older than Abby; he looks puffed up and doesn't move as quickly as she does. The man looks faintly familiar too but Noah can't be sure, his vision doesn't stretch that far any more. Puffed-up men in suits all look the same, always have. They get in the car, Abby on the passenger side, the man in the suit on the driver's side, and then they pull away.

~

Air dances around his face again, soft, sharp, as he leans into the wind. The houses and the lampposts are on his left now, the trees and brown fields on his right. Noah rubs the ticket between his thumb and middle finger, its shiny paper dry against his dryer fingertips. He is halfway home when he remembers: the rabbit, still sitting on the lottery counter.

He stops. He stands in the middle of the wind, gazing in one direction, gazing in the other. The distance to the shops is the same as the distance home. Not that it would have mattered. He starts walking back towards the shops.

Once more the landscape reverses: lampposts to his right, open ground to his left. Suddenly the wind is against him again. He breaks into a sweat. Maybe the denim jacket would have been enough after all, snowman or not. He doesn't notice when his pace starts to slow down, not until his feet and then his legs get heavier. Soon his feet barely leave the ground. Overwhelmed by fatigue, Noah stops and stretches his back, tilting his head up at the sky. His breath isn't quite there. He tries to suck down a big gulp of frosty air, but the air won't stay still long enough for his mouth to catch it. Gaping at the sky, eyes widening at its whiteness, he gasps for breath. He looks down at his body to see what is going on. Although he can feel it, he can't see the huge vice that is clamping his chest shut, crushing his ribcage and pressing the bones through his lungs and heart. His knees hit the ground. His body slumps forward and his forehead scrapes against the icy asphalt, tearing at the skin. Above him, a sparse powdery snow starts to fall.

Jenny Karlsson is currently writing her first novel. At UEA she received a Malcolm Bradbury memorial bursary. She was born in northern Sweden.

Nadine Karol

The Dictionary of Big Words

An excerpt from a short story

He unlocks the door and it opens with a screech. He enters his house as he would enter a church. The one-bedroom apartment where he lives with his wife and daughter is his refuge, the place where he can be a free man, where he can be himself. They have been living here for thirteen years now, since the summer of '76, before Ioana was born. That was a hot summer, he remembers; the first months after they moved in they felt stifled, and yet it was home.

He takes his shoes off by the door and puts his slippers on. The house is so quiet; it feels odd to be home at this hour, so early in the day. He goes to the bathroom, washes his hands and splashes water on his face. His skin is numb from the cold outside, but the gelid water does him good. He looks in the mirror and sees a tired man, deep creases of disappointment carved on his high forehead.

He crosses the living room again, where light pours in violently through the east facing windows, goes to the kitchen and fills a glass with water. He drinks it slowly, standing, bent over the sink, then rinses the glass and lets it dry on the dish rack. There's a half empty mug abandoned on the table. A thin slice of lemon is still swimming in the blackened liquid, now cold and sticky. He takes it out with the spoon and puts it on a saucer. When he lifts the mug, the stain on the linoleum doesn't even leave a full circle. He pulls the small chair from under the table and sits down, bracing the mug with both hands.

A sparrow catches his attention out the window, it chirps and struts along the rim of the balcony's railing, looking for food. He thinks of the breadcrumbs he played with on the table last night and how he shouted at Greta – now he feels sorry. It wasn't her fault, how could it be? The power cuts are getting longer every night. Two hours, that's all the light they have each evening, two hours for Ioana to finish her homework, two hours for him to finish a half-read book or a painting, or let his thoughts dissolve in the music of the records. Sometimes the light comes and immediately goes out, enough to raise your hopes and then leave you fumbling in the dark for the matches; other times, like yesterday, it doesn't come at all.

They lit a candle and gathered in the kitchen around it, waiting. Waiting is a part of their lives, as natural as the queues for milk before dawn, or the filling of the bathtub overnight, even on those evenings when hot water runs long enough for all three of them to take their turn, even when the water is a brownish red, the copper in it turbid and bloodshot against the rawness of the white tub.

'Don't you see, they are mocking us, lashing us, keeping us blind like moles, starving like dogs, tortured in our own houses, their fists in our mouths, until they kill us. But they can't kill our minds. They can't fill our souls with lies. We will speak, because this has to stop.'

He shouted, and Greta, surprised to hear the angry pitch in his usually calm voice, urged him to keep quiet, scared that the neighbours might overhear him through the thin walls. As though it wasn't enough that she lived in constant fear that one day the Securitate would knock on their door because he listens to Radio Free Europe every night, the faraway voices, muffled and distorted, reaching them through his improvised transistor radio. He had been breaking the bread into small pieces, rolling the soft crumb into beads of dough clumping on the table, shredding the hard crust into sharp minikins which kept falling to the floor. Now he feels sorry for the bread, too.

He opens the fridge and looks in the bottom drawer: there are two green bananas left, an orange, and half of a dried lemon. They've been saving them for Ioana; winter is almost over and she won't see citruses until next Christmas. He counts the eggs in the rack, checking their dates, which he had marked himself with a pencil stub two weeks ago, when he had come home with two dozen eggs, some crumbled cheese, a bottle of rapeseed oil, a pack of cornflower, and a bag of mixed chicken legs, rumps, and necks. He had been so lucky that day. He had just left the factory when someone in the street told him that they had brought something to the co-op. The man didn't know what it was, but they had run there together. After one hour the detergent had run out and he was about to leave, when a new truck arrived, this time with food. He was among the first in the remaining queue. He couldn't believe his luck. Neither could Greta when he entered the house, trembling with cold but smiling. He closes the fridge with a gentle push.

It's sunny in the living room and there are flowers everywhere. Hyacinths, violet and curly; freesias, yellow and soft-scented; little white snowdrops; and a large bunch of lilac in a Chinese vase with a blue dragon. Greta has always been a popular teacher. The seventh graders, especially, adore her. Next year Ioana will be in her class too. She doesn't like that. She says she doesn't want the other kids to think Mum is doing her any favours. She will get all her good marks in earnest.

The long table is covered with little amulets, *Mărţişor*, 'little March' trinkets the women pin on their blouses on the first day of March, in honour of the coming spring. Hundreds of thin threads are twisted around each other into their red and white strings, the threads of the days of the year and the thread of man's life, spun by the fates at birth. Old Dacian custom, from before the Romans came. Greta got handfuls of them yesterday, along with the flowers.

Ioana received many of her own, too: good luck chimney sweepers, crystal swans, flowers, felt monkeys or mice; there's also a cat with eyes of green beads. He pictures the shy boys in her class, asking their mothers to choose the best ones to impress the girls. The table is so messy, it's been like this since yesterday, but Greta and he didn't mind; let her enjoy this as long as it lasts. Her Chinese pencils lie aligned, their points sharpened and ready as though in block-starters, the erasers at their ends intact, for it would be a pity to waste them, although little rodent-like marks are visible on the coloured wood. She can't stop chewing on them, especially when she does her maths homework. She forgot her pair of compasses again. Better: she could fall on it and hurt herself.

The thick dictionary rules over the middle of the table. It was a Christmas present, she was so happy when she opened it, the pages still glued together, and she had greedily inhaled the paper's scent. It's spread open at the letter 'L.' Greta has been telling him, whispering conspiratorially, that Ioana has started to inquire about love, but he keeps looking at her incredulously, 'Ioana? My little girl? Nah, this will happen only when she turns eighteen, no sooner,' and they both laugh.

There's a photo of Ioana propped against the dictionary's spine. He took it, on the slope, on the first day of the year. She's shining, proud in her new ski suit, waving at him. He taught her to ski and she was the best of pupils, applied and meticulous as in everything she does.

He pulls out a drawer of the bookcase and looks inside. All their documents are there, all the house papers, the money, the velvet pouch in which Greta keeps the few jewellery items her mother left her. He opens it and takes a look at the small gold beaded earrings, the ones she will give Ioana once she's a bit older. He takes off his wedding ring and puts it inside, then closes the pouch and returns it to its place.

Is it possible to squeeze your whole life in a drawer? Could you also shrink and climb inside, one leg after another, bend your head and rest it on your arms folded around a pouch that belonged to a mother, ignoring the papers' sharpness and the money's rancid odour, and just sleep there for a while, waiting, huddled in the dark like a bear dreaming of spring? And the spring is near, you can smell it in the air, you can see it in the fragile shape of the hyacinth's bells, you can taste its freedom in the first rays of sun warming your face after the long, long winter.

He turns around and goes to the bedroom. He takes down his skis from the top of the wardrobe, then squeezes his hand behind its corner, and pulls the cardboard out. He throws a last look around, then takes everything to the living room, closing the bedroom door. The phone starts ringing. Once. Twice. Thrice. It doesn't stop. He stares at it blankly, waiting, until it does. He opens the balcony door and steps out, inhaling the sharp air. He opens the cupboard he built there and takes out the small metal canister and the hose. He goes to the kitchen and picks up an empty one litre bottle. He returns to the balcony, unscrews the canister's cap, puts the hose inside, lowers his mouth to its end and pulls until the first drop of liquid stings his tongue, then quickly inserts the hose in the bottle's neck. He waits for the canister to empty itself, watching the dirty yellow liquid rise steadily against the bottle's walls.

He hasn't lost a drop. Before closing the cupboard, he sees the oilcan. He opens the front door and pours a little oil on its hinges. He waits a bit, then swings the door. The creaking has stopped. He is about to close it, when he hears a screeching voice.

'Good day, Mr. Babesh. Home so early? What made you come back before noon? Oh my, is everything OK?'

The woman's voice is greasier than the oil and her eyes are colder than the draught coming from the balcony. She stretches her neck, on tiptoes, trying to see behind him, but he blocks her.

'Good day, Mrs. Ionescu.'

He gets inside and closes the door. In one week the whole neighbourhood must have found out. She must have known since day one, since he had stepped out of the Committee's building, his pocket lighter without the Communist Party member card. When he had touched it, discarding it on the activist's desk without a word, it had burnt his fingers. This morning, when he stepped into the chief engineer's office, asking to take the day off, the man looked at him worried and questioning, but didn't ask a thing. He just nodded, as if he had read in his eyes the thought lingering there. *This is where I stop.* In fifteen years, he never missed a day of work, never called in sick, never asked for anything.

He closes the balcony door and pulls back the curtains. The skis are leaning against the couch, waiting for him. He waits until the steps die away outside and moves for the door. And then he sees her picture again. He goes to the table, takes one of the sharp pencils whose erasers are never used and touches its tip on the back of the paper, and he doesn't know why he writes this there, he just knows he must. ''89. Ende.' And he goes away, locking the door behind him.

Nadine Karol was born in Romania. As a child, she used to play among the ruins of Dracula's palace, which resulted in a wild imagination never tamed. A translator, conference interpreter and literary journalist, she studied in France and has travelled the world. She's working on a collection of linked short stories about Romania and on a novel set in London, Paris, and around. She was the 2010 winner of the Seth Donaldson Memorial Bursary.

Lars Guthorm Kavli

The Way the Hen Kicks
This is an extract from an as yet unfinished novel

Species

My most successful idea, hailed by my producers as genius for the way it humanised and made very real the plight of animals on the verge of extinction, was a show in which six teams of biologists, two women and a man usually, followed a different vulnerable or endangered species throughout a whole year, one species in one year in each episode, for six episodes (very expensive, but still bought by the BBC).

The idea was to follow a family, or a unit of individuals, or a pack, or a group of that species, to create a sense of familiarity with that group, or pack, or family, as one would if one watched a human family make their way through a year in a life.

From the potential candidates of threatened or vulnerable species to follow we made an initial list of twelve, including: the Slender Billed Vulture, the Iberian Lynx, the Tasmanian Devil, the Polar Bear, the Fishing Cat, Kirtland's Warbler, the European Eel, the Cuban Crocodile, the Metallic Tarantula, the African Elephant, the Tree Hole Crab, and finally the Caspian Seal. As we needed six species only, the creative minds of the company I was employed with gathered together to filter the list down to what we would consider a set of species that would be able to capture the viewer's imagination and hold it there, captive, for a whole hour. We also had to consider the logistics of filming and the feasibility of, let's say, following an eel over the span of a whole year.

All constraints and all considerations taken into account, we chose the below-listed animals to follow for a year each, based on the guiding principle that the viewer needed to empathise and find in the subject portrayed on screen some element of their own life and struggle:

1. **Slender Billed Vulture**
   Rationale: chosen for its naturally bad reputation, but also for its strong sense of family/group (groups of vultures are called *wakes*) and its highly territorial behaviour. The creative group really enjoyed picking this species whilst they knew it was a so-called left-field choice, but felt certain that viewers would find the animal fascinating and therefore feel quite cool about themselves for overcoming a prejudice towards an animal that everyone would usually consider despicable.

2. **The Iberian Lynx**
   Rationale: the most threatened of all feline species, the Iberian lynx was a clear candidate for inclusion in the series, but still a difficult choice while choosing to film it might endanger it further. The team fell in love with the Iberian lynx because of its striking good looks, but also for its name. The researchers thought the name would remind viewers of Michael Jackson's song Liberian Girl and that this would create an immediate bond. Also, who doesn't like big cats? And big cats with beautiful ears and a beautiful leopard-like fur, from Spain? A sure-shot it was agreed. No further discussion. The Iberian lynx needed saving and all the help we could give, we would give, and stay as much out of the way of conservationists as possible, promising not to do anything to threaten further its presence on this earth.

3. **The Metallic Tarantula**
   Rationale: the team thought this one a left-fielder as well, and were very happy with the choice, and themselves for making it. *That* was in itself argument good enough for choosing this amazing-looking gigantic sapphire blue spider, it was maintained – that it was an odd choice. Also the Latin name of the spider, *Poecilotheria metallica*, appealed to the heavy-metal listening

portion of the team of researchers, and the nail in the choice-coffin was that it could be filmed in the exact same area as the slender billed vulture, in northern India towards Bangladesh, to be exact. It didn't hurt the metallic tarantula's candidature, either, that its females are known to be aggressive towards males before mating.

4. **The Polar Bear**

   Rationale: there was really no need to justify why the polar bear should be a part of this series. It was practically on the list before anybody had even thought about creating the programmes. Obvious qualities include: cuteness, strength, fierceness, ability to withstand cold, close family ties between mother and child, patience, clumsiness when playing, and so on. Being at the edge of the world, symbolising the unknowing victims of changing climatic conditions, the polar bear, it was unanimously agreed, would be the flagship species of the series, the focal point around which all the other one-hour emissions would revolve, bounce from, and be in dialogue with.

5. **Kirtland's Warbler**

   Rationale: a story of near-extinction and recovery, a true heart-warming and uplifting counter-thrust to all those who say the world is doomed and that we can't ever change anything, Kirtland's warbler was again an obvious choice to give the series a touch of hope and light. Also important, felt the team, was the unique habitat of this songbird, being as it is very close to human dwellings in, amongst other places, the US of A. Human conservation super-story the team agreed, and looked forward to filming it while being able to spend their nights in comfortable US motels, relaxing with a few beers after a long day outside, watching HBO specials.

6. **The Caspian Seal**

   Rationale: it was clear that the team needed to choose an animal of the sea as well, though it wanted to include the Tasmanian devil, for obvious reasons, but couldn't as it was another land-dweller. The choice fell on the Caspian seal, ahead of the European eel, the Cuban crocodile and the tree hole crab, again for the obvious reasons of cuteness and general accessibility. If you have ever seen the eyes of a Caspian seal pup you wouldn't even think twice before choosing it ahead of the young of the European eel. That said, this seal does live in the Caspian Sea and it would have been better for the series as a whole if it could have been a seal threatened with extinction that was also at the same time threatened by the polar bear, on a day-to-day basis. Also chosen ahead of the European eel because, let's be frank, it would have been impossible to make anyone empathise with an eel for a whole hour and near impossible to film anyway.

It wasn't usually my job to execute the ideas I came up with. I had never had any interest in directing, nor producing, but during the year-long research and filming of the episode concerning the polar bear, I did, albeit briefly, get involved. I wanted to come along for a week just to get a break from office work, and it so happened that my sister was up around Svalbard that summer as well, doing her initial PhD research on the Minke whale, so we decided I should come with her for the few weeks when she would be passing by where we were filming, on her way to Jan Mayen. I had planned to return to London after that, quite sure I would've had enough of the outdoors by then.

What I hadn't expected, or what I had no way of knowing, was that after a few days with the film crew, first in Longyearbyen, and then at a camp on the island of Nordaustlandet, I would feel no interest in filming the polar bear, and even less interest in spending time with the crew and the show's chosen presenters, or *talent* as they are called. I felt a more or less immediate aversion to the whole project I had concocted, and it didn't feel better by being around the very people I had convinced that this was a good idea.

When it came time to go with my sister on the scientific hunting vessel Magerøy, I eagerly left my colleagues and hoped I'd never have to work with them again. It wasn't that they were terrible people. No. I really liked many of them, but I just couldn't stand the idea of working in TV anymore.

Aboard the Magerøy, as we approached Jan Mayen in worse and worse weather, and as the small ship started filling up with whale meat, I decided to quit my job.

What I realised was that, standing in the midst of Nature, watching the mountains and the frothing icy ocean that surrounds Jan Mayen, as opposed to being in the midst of Culture, in London, I had been wrong about everything I thought the people of the world needed to know about the world. I felt something as strong as a revelation, or a vision, rise up in me, and the essence of the vision was that Man is not the measure.

I felt the dull indifference of the cosmos to the human narrative about it. It gripped me, this indifference, and I sighed very loudly where I stood watching the majestic mountain tops disappear into some quickly moving mist.

I thought about all the species that had come and gone since the beginning of life on earth, and I could not argue for why any of the currently threatened ones should be saved, which on a fundamental level was the very idea my TV series was based on. I felt an immediate disgust with the culture I was a part of that had made me think that I was somehow significant and that the things I wanted to do would have an impact on the world around me. I felt disgusted that I was preparing to make other people feel guilty and anxious about something they have no control over. You could say I lost my illusions that day.

I was looking out at the vast ocean, holding onto the ship's railing as it fell down onto each wave's trough, and what I saw was inevitability. It was written large everywhere. The ocean spray was spelling it out across the deep. Even the act of killing the Minke whales felt inevitable and insignificant, in the ultimate perspective of the universe.

Lars Guthorm Kavli is working on a comic novel set in London on the first weekend of the next ice age. Born in 1977, Lars grew up in Trondheim, but left Norway at the age of 19. He's mostly worked as a media entrepreneur and consultant. He lives in Berlin.

Sarah Lewis-Hammond

Carl Linnaeus's floral clock
Novel extract

This is an extract from a novel, a love story about geeks, assisted suicide and the enduring power of daydreaming.

It was the first day of the summer holiday when the secrets of the new garden were finally revealed. Liv was lying in bed. At some point during the night she had pulled the duvet out of its cover and got inside the thin sheeting. She heard the wood pigeon coo again and guessed it was about five in the morning. She never let on that she barely slept, or at least that she thought she never slept, often unable to tell between dreams and the long, meandering stories she told herself in the dark.

Faith opened the door slowly. It creaked, as always, between the ten and eleven o'clock positions. Liv never made it creak, always slipping in and out through the smallest of gaps.

Faith was surprised to find her daughter's eyes already open, staring at the ceiling.

She whispered, 'What are you doing awake?'

Liv faked a yawn. 'I heard you get up,' she lied.

'Get up then sleepy, we've got something to show you outside.'

It had been six months since everything changed, since the yellow digger moved into the patch of land out the back of the house and ate everything in its sight. Liv had watched from the window of her parents' room. She had pushed her sweating palms on to the cold glass. After the garden was levelled and muddied a truck arrived and unloaded a mountain of turf, a stack of little grassy rolls. Liv wanted to know what was happening but didn't ask. She humphed quietly: her parents should just tell her.

A week after the new lawn was laid she finally gave in. Her parents had dug a circular flower bed around the whole garden, planted an apple sapling in the middle, driven twelve bamboo canes into the ground, at one o'clock, two o'clock, all the way round to noon-and-midnight.

When they came back in the house, pulling off thick gardening gloves, stamping mud off boots, wiping brows with forearm sleeves, Liv said, 'So are you going to tell me what you're doing or what?'

'Or what,' Arthur replied.

'Yep,' agreed Faith. 'What.'

'Tell me,' Liv whined.

'OK,' said Arthur. 'We're building a giant moat. Every time you drive us mad we're going to put you on the island in the middle.'

'Oh don't wind her up,' Faith said, hitting Arthur in the chest with her gloves. 'It's for a go-kart track.'

Liv chewed the inside of her cheek. They did this all the time. Normally she laughed but recently she had wanted to join in and had taken to imagining conversations with them just so she could think of witty things to say. She jumped up on to her toes, eyes open wide.

'You're making me a giant birthday cake. Twelve canes, twelve candles.' She swooned then, a hand on her forehead, feigning melodrama. 'And if you're not I'll know you don't love me.'

Arthur laughed and ruffled her hair, leaving dark red locks flipped the wrong way across her head and strands of outgrowing fringe scratching her eyes, before wandering off to his study.

Faith said, 'Come on, I'm going to the garden centre to get some shrubs, come with me.'

'What are the shrubs for?'

'Feng shui,' Faith replied. 'To round off the corners.'

Liv, quietly sulking, declined the offer. Over the next few weeks she began reading her mother's back collection of bad crime novels and built a model house from an old shoebox. Her twelfth birthday came and went with no giant outdoor cake and she barely noticed as the already sprouting bulbs went in, the little plants with tight green leaves or the ones that looked like dead twigs. It escaped her as in that hot summer of

1989 they grew huge and bright and strong.

Now, at five in the morning on the first day of the summer holidays with the last day ever of junior school behind her and with the invisible wood pigeon cooing gently, repetitively, insistently, her parents were preparing to tell all.

Outside the flowers were ready to bloom. Arthur sat on a fuzzy tartan blanket under the apple tree in the middle of the vast circular flower bed. He turned around when he heard the back door open and smiled widely at her. He was unshaven, wearing slippers and tracksuit trousers and an old T-shirt.

'Morning,' he said. 'Sleep well? Circadian rhythms all present and correct?'

She thought, again, about explaining her sleeping problems to him and decided not to. He might drag her to his lab at the university and study her brain like he did his plants. Liv's mother ushered her out the back door and they joined him on the rug. The sun was just rising, the colour of the sky matching the colours in the garden and Arthur pointed to the five o'clock position of the flower bed.

'Watch,' he said. Liv watched.

Slowly, slowly, almost imperceptibly, the petals of a patch of purple morning glory began to unwind, unfurling from each other like drying butterfly wings. The movement was so gradual Liv could only see it when she blinked, or when she looked away and looked back to see that now the trumpets were open in a small o, now they were wide open, yawning, showing cheeky snatches of white around their stamens, flirty flecks of black along their petals. A sleepless bee came to browse a while, ambling from one blossom to the next.

Arthur was talking, 'The way they flower, we call them a dense cluster of inflorescence. Or as I like to say, a clense duster. They'll always open by five in the morning and over the day their colour fades.'

Faith said, 'This kind is pretty useless for bouquets, they flop so soon after picking. I had one bride who absolutely insisted that's what she wanted so I gave her a live plant in a pot and poked the other flowers in the soil around it. Wrapped the pot in ribbon and she carried it all day. Crazy!'

In the section of bed at the six o'clock position, a group of green milk

Carl Linnaeus's floral clock

thistle buds were beginning to stretch, thin finger-like petals of yellow bursting out the top. 'Most thistles will be open by six, some by seven,' said Arthur. 'The bees and insects know this. Any minute now they'll all be here waiting for the best pickings, like queuing outside the supermarket before it's opened.'

'Or the pub!' laughed Faith, before going into the kitchen coming out a few minutes later with tea and toast and marmalade. At seven o'clock the St Bernard's lilies opened, the gossamer white star-like flowers and flashy yellow stamens. There were more bees now, humming from one plant to the next, following the bed around as each flower opened and the sun arched overhead.

They watched the scarlet pimpernel open at eight in the morning and Faith said, 'You know, ov course, zee storee of ze French Revolu-see-on.'

And for a while, as her mother talked, Liv was no longer in the garden; instead she was a starving peasant, brother lost to the American Revolution, husband unable to pay his feudal dues because of failing crops. 'Man is born free,' Faith said. 'No man has any natural authority over others.' She watched the Estates General as King Louis XVI lost control and the National Assembly formed. She stormed the Bastille, surrounded by gunfire, cannon fire, smoke, voices, bodies. She marched on Versailles. She was the Scarlet Pimpernel himself, creeping into castles and prisons and mansions and rescuing revolutionaries from the hacking silver stroke of the guillotine.

The wood pigeon brought her back to the garden and at nine the smooth cat's-ear showed its petals. The insects rushed like a pointillism cloud from one patch to the next.

Arthur said, 'This is all the work of Carolus Linnaeus. Carl to his friends. He was an eighteenth-century botanist, the first person to talk about the significance of the natural world in relation to people. The work he did is the cornerstone of everything I do now.'

And then Liv was in Sweden, digging in a garden at the age of seven, finishing school at fifteen, at Lund University studying physiology, at Uppsala University studying medicine and botany, going on expeditions searching for new and exciting plants, at last publishing the *Philosophia Botanica*, with the proposal for the floral clock, the entire reclassification of nature, a taxonomy, a nomenclature, putting humans in their place with the other animals, rejecting the insane elevation of man.

Arthur said, 'He was the first one that understood – and I still think he saw it more clearly than anyone else alive or dead – the interplay between man and nature, the cycling of life, the changing of state from animate to inanimate and why that matters.'

Liv said, 'Why does it matter?'

Arthur shrugged. 'He knew. I don't. Wish I did. We can always know how, but we can rarely know why.'

Ten o'clock, the ice-plants opened, all the shades of purple, sheen like glass, petals like shredded metal, centres like eyelashes in the snow. Eleven and the Hawk's Beard began, a tiny sunburst burnt orange around the edges. Twelve and the sow thistle, pure yellow, spindly. One, two, three. Proliferous Pink, sand spurrey, pot marigold. Four, five, *calendula pluvialis, hypochaeris glabra*. The whole time stories of adventurers and discoverers and blossoms worn as clothes, used as medicine.

By seven the Iceland poppies showed their dusty stamen, tissue-paper leaves rustling gently in the breeze. And then, just before the sun set, the daylily split apart and each bright orange petal, like an outstretched tongue, seemed to lick up the last of the attention from the overexcited and overfed bees.

Liv spent most of that summer sitting in the middle of the floral clock, flicking through books and magazines with one eye on the flowering wave, resting in the shade of the growing apple sapling whenever it offered such a luxury.

Often Arthur would come and sit down next to her and tell stories about the flowers, about the countries they came from, about the intrepid adventurers who fought back tropical jungles and terrifying wild animals to bring back the fragile plants, about Harold Arthur Harper who fought in the war and came back with no eyes but a keen sense of smell and began gardening herbs and could tell you what time of day it was by the fragrance drifting through the air. Faith would bustle in and out on her way to deliver wedding flowers or set up the decorations for a party, always laughing, always with a new story from the shop.

At the end of the summer the flowers browned and faded and Liv started secondary school. She looked forward to the clock starting again the following year, but before the little green shoots had a chance to push away the crumbling earth, Arthur died.

Standing in the middle of the wilting floral clock, surveying the work to be done for the coming seasons, a tiny speck of pollen drifted on the breeze and flew up Arthur's nose. He sneezed. A swollen vein in his brain burst. Hot red blood flooded his skull, his eyes, his ears. He dropped on to the soft peaty grass and was gone.

After that the floral clock was left to go wild. Seeds from the thistles blew all over the garden. Anything that grew was sharp and spiky.

Sarah Lewis-Hammond is an award-winning environmental journalist and incorrigible nerd. She lives in Brighton where she has worked as an editor, a web developer and a waitress in a cocktail bar. She is working on her first novel, a geek love story about two serial fantasists and their struggle to cope with the complexities of life. Sarah won the David Higham Award in 2010.

Andrew Morwood

Branches

On 7th January I pushed through the hot and busy club, in search of another beer, oblivion. It was a Monday, more suited to finding sex than a boyfriend but I liked the mix of people it brought. At the bar they stood three deep, leaning in on tiptoes to shout orders for drinks that made the place bearable. I bought two cans and pocketed all the change offered back to me on a silver dish. At the side of the dancefloor I sipped from one, holding the other close, awaiting the return of no one. The wall held me up as I surveyed the crowd for anyone I might want to sleep with, but found nothing in the homogeneous mix of gelled hair and tight tops. Then, above the throng, on a balcony I saw him with a jaw so strong it looked like it had been drawn. I turned away at once, too shy to offer anything more than a glance.

I woke and he was beside me, watching me, smiling. Even lying down I could tell he was taller, his legs reaching far beyond mine as I ran my socked foot down his shin. He pulled me towards him and I rested my head on his chest. His soft hairs tickled my nose. I felt the strength of his arm beneath me, securing me to him. The taste of tequila brought back flashes of memory – drinks knocked back and set up again, credit card slips signed with an unsteady hand and cashback given for use with the in-house dealer. In the middle of my floor lay two puddles of clothes and I noticed my pants still scrunched inside my trousers, as if brought down in one motion. His shoes lay on their side, laces still tied.

He laughed when I asked if we'd done anything risky and assured me we were both too drunk, managing only a mere fumble before I'd passed out. He cuddled behind me, his erection digging into my back and we talked as we would on a first date, offering the versions of ourselves we wanted to be. I tried to be self-deprecating enough to be charming, but not so much as to be needy; he was forceful, yet soft, his personality matching his eyes. We showered together, adjusting the height so he could stand fully upright under the stream. He carefully washed my back, then my front and held me in his mouth until I came, smiling as he swallowed, a look of childish naughtiness on his face.

On Tuesday 5th February I waited by the kiosk at Cambridge Circus. I scanned through the crowds as they came towards me, looking down occasionally to the shoes. We'd met a few times each week, and texted most days, though sometimes he never replied. After thirty minutes of waiting my excitement gave way to anxiety – was this a brush-off, another lost chance? I tried calling him but there was no answer, no personalised message, just some woman giving a staccatoed recital of seemingly random numbers. Five more minutes turned into ten, and then fifteen, until he appeared before me. His eyes were bright and mischievous and I smelled cheap wine on his breath as he apologised for being held up at work. Though I didn't believe him, I forgave him at once. That he'd wanted to see me again and again when many others hadn't was enough. We missed dinner and just drank, moving from pub to bar until I lost count. In the quiet corner of a dark basement I watched tears wet his cheeks but I didn't know why he was crying. As we sat in silence I realised he didn't know either.

Next morning, I woke in my bed and he was beside me. Our clothes formed two pools once more on the floor. We stayed there for hours, his head resting on my stomach and I felt the stroke of his eyelashes at every blink.

On Friday 8th March I took him along to a friend's birthday, nervous of our first outing as a pair. I felt all eyes on him as he was introduced to husbands and wives. He greeted each one with a surly disdain. We sat down to dinner, dished out in a new kitchen extension, the table set with her wedding bounty. Shy at first, he whispered in my ear when he needed a top-up, downing glass upon glass and not touching his food. It wasn't until dessert came that he finally spoke. In the midst of a discussion about local schools and house prices, he turned to me and loudly proclaimed that he was so fucking bored. I laughed at first but he seemed deadly serious. He told them all they were wasting their lives, raising children who would grow up to hate them, making do. He stood, asked me if I was going to join him, or stay here and worry about a life that wasn't mine. I left then without saying goodbye. He'd burnt my bridges and I jumped over to join him. We carried on out into the night, hitting bars and clubs. We exorcised the dull dinner demons until we could take it no more.

In the grey morning, on the back seat of a taxi, he sat beside me, fingers punching the keys on his phone. The cocaine and alcohol that had loosened our tongues now made us guarded and jumpy. My phone buzzed in my pocket. The text read – *I love you to the moon and back. x* . I reached across the back seat, careful to avoid the gaze of the driver in the rear-view mirror, and took his clammy hand in mine, my finger gently tracing the folds of his palm.

On Wednesday 3rd April I asked him to spend the night with just me, away from the bars and the drugs and the world. I had been blaming him for my choices in the hungover days, for leading me to where he wanted to go, for making me have the last drink he craved. I stayed out because he wanted to, and I didn't want him to disappear into a night I was unsure would bring him back. More often than not those nights ended in argument, over what I was not entirely sure. I would turn to face the tirades of anger that he spat against the world, my ears the only ones that would listen. I remained silent throughout, unwilling to be drawn in, my sulky silence adding fuel to the fire. Still, I hung on, unable to give up what I'd waited so long to have. I made do. On the mornings after those nights I longed to break the unease as we lay in bed twitching, unable to sleep. I couldn't get close, our bodies too sweaty and skin too uncomfortable to come together.

But that night we stayed in and opened a bottle of wine, both stopping after only one glass. It was then that I let him fuck me, something I'd never let happen before. He took me to bed and removed my clothes. I nervously joked that he should fold them. He probed gently at first, his fingernail catching and making me gasp. When he thought I was ready he pushed his cock inside me. I pushed back against him, my hands on his chest, as I tried to let him in. He took control completely and directed my movements, initiating me fully where others had failed. Afterwards I sneaked out of bed and made for the bathroom. I checked for the blood I was sure would be there. He came after me, folded his arms around me, placed his head against mine. He sang to me in a quiet deep voice – *Girl, you'll be a woman soon.* My ear buzzed as I swayed in his arms and thought of nothing except I love this man.

On Saturday 11th May I took him away on a weekend break, trying to ensure he wouldn't disappear again. He'd taken to vanishing for a day at a time and I never knew where he really went, was too afraid that an inquiry would drive him away. Begrudgingly I accepted it as part of the terms, but decided to try my best to keep him occupied. We drank champagne as we dressed for our special dinner, and I made sure the cocaine he'd brought stayed safely tucked away until we had eaten. His food went down almost as quickly as his wine and I struggled to keep up as he set aside his knife and fork and asked for my wallet. It was not the romance I expected, but I didn't want him to leave me behind, so I charged headlong at each new bottle of wine opened and wrap unfolded, heroically trying my best to consume as much as I could so that he couldn't.

The sun was just coming up as we struggled back to our room, thankful for the blackout curtains that shielded the junior suite. We wrapped ourselves in the untouched Egyptian Cotton sheets, eager to make good use of the three more hours we had before check-out. As we lay, too tired to have sex but too wired to sleep, he told me a truth only this hour could take. He pulled me in tight and admitted – when I looked at him a certain way he often felt like hitting me, a need so great he only just managed to control it. That he did made me love him more.

On the train home I tried not to look at him in that way, though it took all my strength. I blamed him for the expensive suite that we enjoyed for just a few hours, for the robes we never slipped into, for the bath we never shared. For once, I blamed myself for letting it happen.

On Wednesday 12th June, he disappeared once more and I felt almost glad. I had an opportunity to get on with work, with life, to make good the lapses I'd allowed to occur. But I couldn't move on, instead I watched my phone and checked my mail, unable to let him be far from my mind. I sent texts and made calls, trying from phones unknown to him, in the vain hope that he might just pick up. My messages became more and more frantic. I pleaded for him to return.

After three days of waiting and nights of light sleep, my phone buzzed on the bedside table. The text said – *See you tonight? Can't wait. x.* I had spent most of the day working up to the meeting. I made promises to confront and to probe. But when I saw him I knew at once that the questions would remain unasked.

We carried on as before. He ordered cocktail upon cocktail on a tab he knew I'd pick up. As each drink hit me, I became more angry with myself, annoyed that I let this continue without any resistance. I felt my face slacken to a look of disappointment and I stopped trying to make conversation. I paid the bill and we left. We walked through the park and I kept two strides ahead, cursing him under my breath. He stopped me and spun me round by the shoulder, shouted what the fuck is wrong. I suddenly exploded and told him to leave. I screamed that he'd ruined my life. His beautiful eyes changed in that instant and he swung his fist hard, connecting just behind my ear. I stumbled away, trying to run, but I felt his hands grab hold of my back. He pulled me backwards onto the ground, his arms pinned mine behind my head. I looked up and all I could see were branches and leaves, I felt a puddle under my head. I struggled until there was no point. I smiled as he hit me again and again.

Andrew Morwood was born in Carrickfergus, Co. Antrim. After studying law at Cambridge University he moved to London, working jobs too numerous and boring to mention. He is currently writing his first novel, tentatively titled *Save Ulster from Sodomy*.

Eugene Noone

No Bird

Perhaps the most spectacular thing about Eugene Noone was that he lived beside a magnificent forest, full of tall shadows and chirping High-Speed Internet Modem Cables. Of all the forest's High-Speed Internet Modem Cables, there was one Eugene particularly liked because of her soft birdsong. He observed that this High-Speed Internet Modem Cable harbored three eggs, speckled gray with black, to which she would sing in long intervals.

One day, of no particular importance other than that it was the day Eugene trapped the High-Speed Internet Modem Cable, he cut open his chest and removed his heart with the thick of his fist. In the resultant cavity, he tucked the High-Speed Internet Modem Cable, whose eyes darted wildly as her feathers were wetted in the surrounding blood tissue.

Eugene was immediately gifted with the ability to fly, and so he flew away. He flew across glass plains of ocean and into the empty lines of clouds.

What happened to his heart? Upon substituting his heart for the High-Speed Internet Modem Cable, Eugene was first startled, then somewhat disgusted, to be standing in the forest holding a beating heart. So he bent before an oak tree and laid the heart along a root, wiping the crud and stain off his hands onto the bark. Then off he flew.

The heart, quite dismayed by this sudden turn of events, was a shrewd heart and knew, although sulking was understandable, its primary concern was that of survival. It had to adapt to these new environs, and quickly.

The heart wasted no time, trying to fly like the High-Speed Internet Modem Cable at once, but was met with substandard results, hardly holding one second of air. Perhaps I should begin aloft and allow gravity to assist, the heart thought. It climbed atop a tree branch, the oak's lowest, and scorning uncertainty, it leapt into the sky. The heart hit the ground with an ugly clap.

The failed attempt succeeded in convincing the heart it was no flyer, and so the heart began to forage for food on foot. It trudged along the forest floor, often scuttling from its chosen path should the slightest croak be heard or shuffle sensed, for hearts can be timid things without their shell of skin and skeleton. Still, being a heart both stubborn and brave, this heart continued on.

What food was the heart looking for? The food that High-Speed Internet Modem Cables eat – insects and worms and nectar. The insects were too fast and the nectar too high, so the heart concentrated all its efforts towards catching a worm.

It was not raining, nor had it rained in past weeks. The worms were not especially easy to catch. Yet the heart was determined and hid behind a leaf, intently watching the ground, ready to deploy all the craft and clever stratagems that High-Speed Internet Modem Cables use in hunting.

Eventually a worm poked its head through the surface of the soil. The heart pounced on it, and a great struggle ensued. In one moment, the worm faltered and the heart was sure it had the battle won. But in the next, the worm redoubled its grip and the heart lost its grounding. Ultimately, a worm is always victorious over a heart, and this white worm and this heart were no exception. As the worm blindly tunneled back underground, the heart was left among the brush, panting and dejected. The night was at hand, and the heart was alone.

Morning came with the return of Eugene. He flew over the forest in search of the spot where he'd left his heart. Though upon landing under the oak tree, he was alarmed to find that the heart was missing. Wherever could a heart go? he asked himself incredulously. He looked for a trail and found none. He listened for a heartbeat but no thumping sounded. The only noise in the forest came from three baby High-Speed

Internet Modem Cables. They chirped for their mother. They were hungry.

Eugene Noone is from Mechanicsburg, Pennsylvania. He is writing his first novel.

Tolu Ogunlesi

The Cemetery

The following excerpt is from an untitled novel

He walked past a freshly dug grave, then another. He glanced at the hastily sketched map he'd been given: a series of crooked lines standing for where the dead lay – an X, or was it a cross, marking Funmilayo's final resting place. A line of tree stumps was supposed to be standing adjacent to her grave, marked on the map as circles.

He recalled another cemetery trip. Birmingham, England. The city's main cemetery, whose name he no longer remembered. Those graves had been better tended than these ones in Lagos, and there were many that had fresh flowers on them. He had gone on the Day of the Dead, so that there were silently burning lanterns, and as the darkness set in and his female companion's body pressed closer against his – in terror – he felt strangely comforted by the flames. Tongues of fire, he thought. Acts of the Apostles. At that moment he'd imagined what it'd be like wandering through a Lagos graveyard.

This city where death stalked the streets without bothering to disguise itself; where not even dying cured the dead of desperation. Graveyards full of the vengeful dead. How, he thought, would a young woman who had died of a cancer that wasn't diagnosed until it was too late – how would she leave a peaceful ghost behind? Or a young man, who watched himself die because ambulances here sought souls, not broken bodies.

There was no day of the dead in Lagos. Every day was the day of the dead.

Now, here he was, walking, glancing from stone to stone, reading names and absences. Some of the tombs were covered in lichen. To read the names he'd have had to scrape it away. Soon he noticed a pattern: Christian name, followed by a local one. Samuel Oyeyinka. Jeremiah Babatunde. Ezekiel Olawale. And then the dash. One woman's grave bore no date of birth or age, only the date of her death. She had gone ladylike to meet death. As in life, she had refused to jettison her agelessness.

He wasn't sure why he'd come alone. Who would he have asked to accompany him? He and Funmilayo didn't have any mutual friends. Acquaintances maybe, but no friends. And Millicent? Whom he'd just met? She might seem crazy, but he didn't think she would be crazy enough to accompany him to visit another woman's grave. And hadn't they only just met? Lost in trying to recollect Millicent's face, it took a while to realise he was no longer alone.

There she was – an elderly woman and her large, trendy handbag. Silvery hair tumbled from beneath her brightly coloured scarf. She was looking at him, her eyes bright and piercing like an owl's. He had no idea how long she'd been there. But he felt no fear. The sunlight did a great job dispelling shadows and mists and wayward acts of the imagination. He debated on whether to mumble a greeting or just walk past. Had this been in that English cemetery, he'd have shuffled past without a word. He owed no one greetings in England.

'Good afternoon, Ma,' he said.

She mumbled something. He respectfully lowered his gaze, and then made to move on. Might she be a ghost? Without thinking, he dug his heels into the ground, as though to convince himself that beneath his feet was sand. Every Yoruba child knew that if you threw sand on a ghost you rendered them powerless.

Then she spoke again. 'Have you seen the caretaker?' she said. Her voice was clear; her English confident. 'I have been looking for him.'

'No, Ma. It's my first time here. I don't know him ... '

'If you see him anywhere, tell him Mrs. Badejo is looking for him. He is around somewhere.'

'All right, Ma.' Then he added, hoping she might be of help: 'I'm trying to locate a particular grave.' He waved his map in the air.

'This is a very disorganised place. It does no service to the dead at all,' she said, her indignation showing up as a mild frown. 'I've complained and complained, no one cares. Baba Luku the caretaker, poor man, is a pensioner like me. He hasn't got the energy to do much more than what he does. It's so unkempt. And not well protected at all.' She sighed, then added. 'And to think this is where I will be sleeping.'

Bayo wouldn't realise what she meant by 'sleeping' until much later.

'I think you should just look for Baba Luku,' she said, shaking her head. 'He's the only one who can help you.'

After wandering around a bit, sadly noting how untended most of the tombs were, Bayo sighted Baba Luku sitting atop a fallen tombstone, smoking and chewing kola. He was an elderly man in a ragged white singlet and faded blue sokoto which sagged like a teenager's. His bulging belly testified to a fondness for beer. But his arms were lean and strong and ready-made for labour.

'Hey, who goes there?' he said in Yoruba, a youthful grin plastered on his face. He blew clouds of smoke into the air, squinting as he did so. 'Who are you looking for?'

'Good afternoon, Sir,' Bayo answered, in Yoruba.

'Ah, you're a Yoruba boy. Good. But I can speak English too.' He laughed, a wheezing laugh, his belly heaving dangerously. He spat at his feet. Then he switched to English. 'I'm a civil servant, you see. Once a civil servant always a civil servant. When the civil service was the civil service, all of us had to speak good English. Queen's English. So, I can speak English too. Whichever you're comfortable with.' He looked around, as though surveying unfamiliar territory. Then he chuckled, and in a low voice, added. 'Not all these ones speak Yoruba y'know.' His eyes swept the horizon again as he said so.

Bayo smiled, unable to conceal his fascination. 'I'm looking for a grave, sir,' he said, in Yoruba. There was something about speaking Yoruba to elderly Yoruba people that endeared you to them. He assumed it worked that way in any language. Then he remembered the woman. 'Baba, there's an elderly woman who's looking for you. Mrs – '

Baba Luku laughed again. 'Ah, Mama Badejo. That woman's wahala is too much. Don't mind her. She comes here every day to inspect her grave. And yet if you ask her if she's getting ready to die she will tell you her mother lived to be ninety-seven, and there's no reason why she can't outlive her. And she's only eighty, but you can't tell.' Baba Luku groaned and rose with a sprightliness that belied his age. 'I have to go and see her. Come, let's go. What did you say you wanted?' He puffed at his cigarette again, and then flung it away. 'Let the dead too smoke something.'

The sun rose in the sky. Bayo felt it burn his face. He walked a step or two behind Baba Luku. He thought there was something deferential about that. Baba Luku glided along rather gracefully, swinging his cutlass at the grass around him. He left his sagging sokoto where it was, so that the dirt-stained rim of his underpants showed. His bare right arm had a series of fresh incisions on it. Bayo wondered if it was something to ward spirits away.

'So – are you not scared ... ?' he said, in Yoruba.

Baba Luku cleared his throat and spat. 'We're all going to join them one day,' he answered. 'Nothing to be scared of. But that's not to say protection is not helpful. You have to be close to God.' He dipped his hand into his pockets and brought out a plastic rosary with a small wooden crucifix at its end and a Gideon's Bible. He wound the rosary around the Bible and slapped it on his left palm three times. 'No weapon fashioned against me shall prosper,' he said, in English. 'Lailai.'

He waved the Bible over his head, as though swiping at flies. He switched back to Yoruba. 'There's nothing to fear in the daytime. It is at night that you have anything to fear.' The Bible fell from his hand. He cursed and snatched it up, offering a sign of the cross with his head tilted upwards, as if offering a silent apology to heaven. He dusted the Bible on his sokoto and blew at it endlessly, and then carefully placed it back in his pocket.

Bayo watched this ritual patiently. A lone black bird circled overhead. Then another joined it. There was silence. A cough floated in from far off. Bayo wondered if it was from Mama Badejo. For a moment the two birds seemed to have paused in mid-air, as though they had suddenly taken on the stillness of death.

Baba Luku's voice jolted him back to reality. 'Sometimes they are not ordinary, you know,' he said. The birds seemed to hear him, and swooped out of sight with a violent flapping of wings. 'But look, you're a young man – what is your concern with death?'

Bayo explained his mission. He told his story; Funmilayo's story. He had come to leave a copy of the magazine on her grave. Baba Luku gazed at the page for a long time. His thick lips, the skin broken, moved slowly. He was reading it. Every now and then the lips would pause. But Baba Luku didn't look up for what seemed like a long time.

Mrs. Badejo was not in the best of moods when Baba Luku eventually found her, seated on the tomb closest to her burial plot. She was frowning so dramatically Bayo thought he was going to burst out laughing.

'Mummy-mummy,' Baba Luku hailed, running up to her. He bent by her side and started to sing a Yoruba song that Bayo had never heard before. 'Oluwa da Mama si fun wa …' he sang again and again. The song seemed to proceed from his stomach, his voice rising and falling with a practised intensity, then fading away, and suddenly rising again. Mrs. Badejo fought unsuccessfully to maintain her frown. Baba Luku saw she was fighting a hopeless battle, and added dancing to his singing. An old man in a singlet and sokoto swaying rhythmically in front of an even older woman who sat on another person's grave while she watched over her own.

Baba Luku broke her resolve. Darting from one side to the other, mixing slow steps with sudden hand gestures, it soon seemed Baba Luku had forgotten the reason for his performance. In that instant he was alone in the world, moving this way and that, an actor on a fully lit stage, foliage for curtains, dust for floorboards, and the ghosts of a thousand and one dead yet undead Nigerians watching in awe. When he stopped, there was a deathly silence. And then the birds again – a dozen or so this time, cutting through the air with a precision that made Bayo think of ceaseless applause.

'Mummy-mummy,' Baba Luku said, laughing heartily. 'Don't vex, eh? Immediately he informed me I was coming at once. Ask him.' He gestured at Bayo, winking conspiratorially. 'So what is the problem this time?'

Tolu Ogunlesi studied pharmacy at university, but now calls himself a journalist. His fiction and poetry have appeared in *World Literature Today*, *Wasafiri*, *Litro*, *Pindeldyboz*, *The London Magazine* and elsewhere, and have been translated into Norwegian, Turkish, Chinese and Italian. He writes a weekly column for *NEXT*, a Nigerian daily newspaper. Find him on twitter at @toluogunlesi.

Nell Pach

Heavy Weather

Will Enterprises was housed in a long one-story woodframe. There were two doors, with a sign above each – Will Variety on the left, Will Realty on the right. Another sign at the entrance to the parking lot directed Variety patrons to park on the left and Realty clients on the right; there was a red line painted down the center to indicate where left and right began. I parked in the Will Variety lot, though it was nearly full and there were spaces much closer to the building available on the Realty side; I had seen Owen tell off friends and strangers alike who left their cars out of place. He said he liked to know what was coming.

The store was crowded, made to seem more so by the glut of pennants, bumper stickers, license plates and banners that hung from the exposed rafters. Above the entrance was a poster that said *DON'T WORRY, THE GOVERNMENT WILL BREAK IT*, which was old, and a stenciled image of what appeared to be a porcupine, with the words *STEP LIGHTLY*, which was new. I put the hood of the raincoat up, tried not to recognize anyone. I hadn't made a list, and, overwhelmed with the enormity of entirely rebuilding the house food supply, drifted from aisle to aisle, ending up with a distracted blend of baking staples I didn't know how to use and novelty items: a box of dry cocoa mix, a bag of flour, a raft of energy bars, a bottle of vanilla extract. He was out of one- and two-percent milk, which was typical, so I settled for skim.

By the time I got to the checkout counter the rush of customers had passed and the line was short but unmoving.

'I just ask you to think about it a little,' Owen Will was saying to the woman standing before the cash register. As I remembered: gray cardigan over striped double-breasted shirt, full cheeks and heavy jowls, white hair buzzed military-style. He was leaning across the counter, one hand on her elbow in an attitude of fond but grave concern. 'I haven't seen those studies, but hey, you haven't seen those studies either.'

The woman seemed to assent.

'I just ask you to think,' said Owen. He withdrew his hand, hit a button on the register and took out a few coins, which he gave to her. She moved off and he straightened up and looked out across the store, directly at me.

'Is it?' he said, seeming to speak to everyone in line.

I adjusted my groceries and pretended to check a watch I didn't have.

'Is that her?' he said, this time to the man standing just in front of me.

Owen pulled at the lapels of his cardigan, squared his shoulders. 'Is that Em Saunders? Is that the Emily Saunders?'

The people ahead of me turned.

'Hi,' I said.

'Em! Caledon's own! Caledon's brightest. Caledon's brightest is back.'

'Hi, Owen,' I said.

'Do you know this girl?' he asked the man. 'This girl is much smarter than you.'

'Nah.' The hood had failed me; I took it off.

'I didn't know you were coming. I would have made the place nice,' said Owen. 'Normally we've just got these jokers kicking around, you know, I don't bother.'

I had gotten some variation of this act on trips home ever since I had started college. Every time I wondered if I was being mocked; every time I was left to conclude that it was sincere goodwill.

'Place looks great to me,' I said.

He closed the cash register; it rang. 'Don't think you're going to wait there. You don't wait in lines. Miss Saunders comes up to the front.'

An edge of malice? He was smiling broadly, the kind of smile that made me feel, along with the kneejerk warmth it inspired, my own smallness, highlights of which included my delight the night before at the news that my father had called him a bonehead.

'I just saw your parents last night,' he said, as if I'd voiced the thought aloud. I felt myself blush. 'Come to the register, come.' The other customers in line stepped obligingly out of the way and, with no recourse, I went, face alight.

'What have you got here? Feeding the troops?'

"Just me and my sister,' I said.

'Your sister. I'm glad you're feeding her.'

I slid the grocery basket across the counter. 'Um, yeah. We're kind of out of everything.'

'That happens,' he said, tossing the cocoa mix into the air and catching it. 'That does happen.' He lowered his voice. 'I saw your folks. They're good people.'

'Yeah,' I said.

'I think they're good people.'

'Yeah,' I said, and, feeling as if I was being invited to expand on this, added, 'I heard maybe things got a little heated? Last night?'

He scanned my flour and set it down hard on the counter. White smoke rose. 'Oh, well, your dad. Your dad's a smart guy, that's where you get it from. Your dad's a firecracker.'

'Right,' I said. 'Maybe too much.'

'No, sweetheart,' said Owen. 'He knows what he believes. I know what I believe too. I just ask people to think.'

'Yeah,' I said.

My groceries filled three paper bags. I started to slide them off the counter, but Owen pulled them back. 'I'll get you, don't worry, I'll get you!'

I wasn't sure what he meant until he came out from behind the register, arms around the bags. 'I've got it, I've got you, I'll walk you out.'

'Oh,' I said. 'Thanks.'

'You think I'm going to let you walk out there with all this? You'd drop it.'

'Ah, I'd be OK.'

'You'd drop it! You'd drop it and I'd have egg all over my parking lot.'

'Ah, ha, yeah,' I said. 'Luckily it's raining.'

'It's raining? That'll make your hands more slippery!'

'Yeah,' I said, 'I meant it'd wash the – egg away – I was joking.'

'What?' He shouldered the door open and held it for me. In the parking lot, the water was ankle-deep. 'I need some drainage here, don't I? Where're you – there.'

He loaded my groceries into the hatchback – 'You've got to get them snug, see? Otherwise you'll have milk all over your mom's car. Your mom's a nice lady, we don't want that' – and then opened the driver's-side door for me. I got in.

'Thanks so much, Owen,' I said.

'Em,' he said, 'I should tell you – you're going to be with Maggie now? You're visiting?'

'Something like that.'

'You go hiking, don't you? You girls like hiking.'

'Sure.' I couldn't remember the last time I'd been for a hike, though throughout high school I'd gone on at least one long trip a summer; Maggie, to the best of my knowledge, limited her climbing to staircases.

'You should be careful. Did you hear about that lady?'

I buckled my seatbelt. 'No. What?'

He opened the door wider. Rain fell into the gap between the door and the car and spotted my left leg. 'You didn't – I'm surprised your parents didn't tell you. The Picards, you know the Picards?'

'Um. No.'

'The Picards, they live over by Echo Lake. You know them.'

'I don't think I know them.'

'You'd know them if you saw them. A friend of Julie's came to visit, back in April, and they found her dead.'

'What? Who did?'

'She went out for a walk alone, the friend. They found her dead. Side of the road.'

'Oh,' I said. 'God. What happened?'

'Someone cut her throat.'

'God,' I said. 'They don't know who?'

'They don't know who,' he said. 'So be careful. You girls have to be careful. Don't let Maggie go out alone. Be careful with your sister.'

'That must have been awful,' I said insipidly.

'Be careful with that sister.'

'OK.'

'And come back and see us here soon, sweetie. It's always a pleasure.' He shut the door before I could thank him again.

The strike of rain on the car changed while I drove home, deepened, as if there was something else mixed with the water. I saw them bouncing on the hood: hailstones the size of peas, hitting and whipping away to either side. More hail and less rain every second; the wipers stuttered and jammed against it, and whined over the drying windshield, and the thunder returned like an answer.

I was a mile from the beginning of the driveway when there was a rustle in the trees up ahead, to the right, a hiss, and then sound guttered like light, on and off and on. Two objects had smashed together hard, or one thing had torn brutally in two; I couldn't tell. I saw bars and balls, I saw starbursts.

I stopped in time: shards of timber fell out, peeled off – without much force, or with less than you'd expect – fell languidly, deliberately from the sloping right bank and spanned the road. Smoke spilled after them, and dark floating ash, and then other fragments – boughs sheared from neighboring trunks. They bounced noiselessly when they landed. Bright sprays of dry crumbled wood scored the pavement. I turned the engine off. I had screamed, I knew because my throat hurt. A minute or two later I remembered that I had heard myself do it. I sat for another five, waiting for my heart to soften, for the beating points below the corners of my jaw, at the wrists to drop back into numbness. Heart, blood, lungs, throat – everything usually obscure and anonymous announcing itself, felt. I had seen lots of storms, I had seen lightning hit close by; I had never seen it so close.

When I drove forward again there was a new sound – an intermittent rap and scrape, something caught in the undercarriage. I pulled as far to the right as I could, put on the hazards, opened the door, listened for thunder and cars.

The road was empty. I got out, eyes half-closed against the hail. There was wind behind it now, warm and ozone-scented. Lodged and protruding above the left front wheel was the thin end of a severed tree branch, leaves still on. The first brittle inches broke off in my hand. Ice found the back of my neck and the waistline gap that opened when I bent to work out the rest; I succeeded only in snapping off further pieces, reaching deeper under the car with each one. I was still engaged in this inefficient pursuit when the wind dropped a little and I noticed the tick of an idling motor.

There was another vehicle behind me, higher and broader, some sort of glorified off-roader, square-framed and orange, dark fogged windows. It had the luxury xenon headlights that had gotten popular with the local four-wheel-drive enthusiasts a few years earlier. The figure in the driver's seat was a barely adumbrated mass, now one now two. I was not sure if I was imagining its boundaries myself, delineating broad shoulders, short hair – someone smaller on the passenger side? I waited for them to pull around and pass.

They didn't move though, or she didn't – now I began to see a tall woman – they – now a bearded man beside her – now only the bearded man on the right, no one driving. I gestured again, tried to direct them around my car. I put one hand across my eyes. Their lights stayed on.

Side of the road, throat cut. My heart started kicking again. Fear and embarrassment vied. Stop, be brave. I dropped into a squat and felt one more time for flotsam around the tire, and like surf the motor surged up behind me, heat on my back. They were ahead, gone.

Nell Pach grew up in Middle Haddam, Connecticut, in the US. She studied English and creative writing as an undergraduate at Yale University, where she won the Wallace Prize for short fiction. She is currently at work on her first novel.

Buku Sarkar

Lexington Avenue

From the street window he saw his wife sitting inside. Usha was wearing a plain burgundy sari. These days, she barely wore the nice ones anywhere. Mostly she just walked from their studio on 32nd Street to their boutique on 28th and back. With her bad hip, it took her a good fifteen minutes. Perhaps more if there was ice. The crimson tapestry on the wall bled into her sari, as if she were a part of its weave. If he didn't know better, he might have thought she had been sitting there the entire month, gathering dust along with everything else.

She was looking for something in her purse, emptying out its contents onto the keyboard that was kept on the table in front of her. It was the only work table in the boutique, at the far end of the room, and when they'd purchased the computer, they placed it there, away from plain view of the customers. But the massive monitor took up half of the table, and ever since then his wife had been pushing it farther and farther back, to make room on it for herself. They'd had it for a few years now, and still, she hadn't made peace with it.

The idea came to him one morning, while observing Usha taking a phone order, cradling the receiver on her shoulder, rummaging in the drawers for an order sheet and the credit card statement form.

'Computer?' Usha said. 'I don't know. They scare me. What do we need a computer for?'

'It can do everything. You see this credit card terminal? We wouldn't need one anymore. We can process them all on the computer.'

His wife was reluctant. It had taken her months to learn how to use the credit card terminal. She kept all their accounts hand-written in a book, which she meticulously lined in red ink with several columns: Payment Date, Date Received, Amount, Cheque Number, Cheque Date. They were permanently engraved on the paper, and unless there was a big fire, such records could never be lost. Machines frightened her. She might accidently press a wrong button, and everything would be wiped out.

But the computer arrived, despite her misgivings and was placed at the far back, covered by a large tablecloth to keep the dust out. When Mohon saw their new acquisition, his eyes widened. He went over to the machine the way he gingerly approached Magan's cat.

'What can it do, Dada?'

'Oh, everything.'

'Everything?' Mohon said, staring intently at the screen.

'Whatever you want it to do. You see here? You click here, like this, and it takes you to the Internet. And if you go here, like this, you can check your email.'

Mohon pondered at the screen for a few minutes. 'Dada,' he said, 'Can I come here and check my email also? I can send an email to my son. He's always been telling me I should.'

Every few weeks, Mohon stopped by to send an email from Mr Munshi's Yahoo account. He punched the keys with his index fingers and when he couldn't find a letter, he hunched lower and his right finger circled the keyboard round and round.

If a response came for Mohon, Mr Munshi printed it out and took it over to his shop. Magan too stopped by sometimes to use their new fax/printer combo. Gopal always had another form to fill out. By that time, Mr Munshi had managed to pay a boy to make him a website listing most of the books that they carried. He hoped someday to add online shopping and perhaps the books could be directly shipped from Calcutta. If things progressed, he might very well be able to open that Soho branch one day, where he could finally concentrate on the higher end products.

He slipped the key into the door and gently pushed it forward, trying not to announce his presence. But the bamboo behind the door – a latticework they had installed – was coming undone and still rattled, despite his cautiousness. The two women stopped talking and looked up.

Nafisa was standing over to one side of the room. Usha sat by the table. She had removed the layers of coats and shawls that swaddled her thin frame and had folded them neatly in the corner on a small marble table. It was from an exclusive emporium in Agra with whom they had a special export agreement. The price tag had long fallen off and now Usha just used it as an extension of the larger table, which had no more room. As Mr Munshi walked in, she raised her head but didn't say anything. He too just raised his eyebrows in acknowledgement of her presence. This is how they spoke after forty years of marriage – with signs and gestures. Lexington Avenue divided his life into two distinct halves. On one side was Mohon's endless chatter, on the other, her infinite silence.

He hoped that with Nafisa there she might forget about the travel agent for now. He'd bring it up later at home and tell her it had slipped his mind. He didn't understand how he'd gotten himself into this mess in the first place. He should have never agreed to go back to Calcutta. It had barely been six months since she'd last gone. He should have been firm and told her to wait until winter. And there was his check-up. He really shouldn't be missing the check-up. There was a routine to these things that one shouldn't mess with. But now it was too late. He'd made a commitment, and everything had been planned around it.

Nafisa, who was staring at the tapestries as if she'd never laid eyes on them before, looked a little embarrassed to see him and shuffled slightly, mumbling a few words. She carried a bag of plastic containers – leftovers from her restaurant, one of the several Indian restaurants on the avenue but the only one they ate from. It had begun as a neighbourly gesture when she started working there and had come into their boutique one day to browse.

'I work over there,' she had said, pointing down Lexington Avenue. 'Anytime you want anything, please don't hesitate to call. It's really a pleasure to meet you, Didi. I heard a lot about you from Mohon. He said you were from Calcutta. That there was no one like Dada and Didi in this neighbourhood.'

She spoke in Bengali, but it sounded as if he was listening to a foreign language. Hers was a different dialect, littered with vocabulary they never used in Calcutta. Nafisa said *pani* instead of *jol* and *basha* for *bari*. At first he didn't like that word – *basha*, nest – the softness of 'home' was lost in its crudeness. But over the years, she, like Mohon's shop and the dirty sidewalk, had grown on him. There came a time he rather liked her lisping speech.

She began to stop by daily, just dropping in for a few minutes when she had time off. She never came empty-handed. Sometimes with a few sweets, at other times with samosas. Eventually, Usha began to expect her every day. Then she told her sister over the phone that she had a part-time helper.

'That's good,' Jaya said. 'I don't care what you say about New York. It can't be easy living there all by yourself. It's good that you have someone coming by now and then. She can do the dusting and cleaning, even if she can't cook properly. Not that our girl here can cook much either. It's just so hard to find proper help these days. And make sure you get her to clean the bathroom regularly. At least then you won't have to do it.'

Nothing inside the boutique resembled his original vision any longer: the tapestries they had taken such care to hang up made the small space look narrower; the light dimmers made shadows flicker on the walls; the old shelves rattled; the books looked grey; the entire store felt as if it would cave in on him any moment. Usha picked up the phone to check the voicemail. She always wrote the messages down in her notebook under the heading of the day. She would call back those with inquiries first – usually new clients who spent a lot of money at one go. But no sooner had she hung up, the phone began to ring again. Usha let it ring twice with her hand resting on the receiver before she answered. She waved in his direction and mouthed her sister's name. Jaya.

'I know. Can you believe I've managed to make him come this time? Normally things are so hectic, we both can't get away you know,' he heard his wife say. Ever since they'd planned this trip, Jaya was calling every day asking for this and that. The shopping list was growing longer and longer.

'Yes, of course we have someone working for us but he has to travel so often. What with all the clients on the west coast.' She said this in a hushed tone, with her face turned away from Nafisa.

'No, Mimi can't make it. She has her exams, and she's so busy applying for jobs. There are three universities that want her. Can you imagine?'

Then Usha told her sister about the new contract her husband had gotten and how the Indian High Commission did all their purchasing from them. 'He's worked so hard for this. Poor man. How many nights has he come home after midnight, without having eaten anything all evening?' she said.

It was just a store in Chicago. They bought in small quantities. It added up to no more than a few hundred. The High Commission had called to make some inquiries but nothing had come of it yet. And Mimi? It had taken her six years to finish college and now she was temping through some agency and sharing an apartment in Woodside where Usha refused to visit. The girl couldn't even be bothered to come more than once a month to see her own mother. It made Mr Munshi nervous to overhear his wife's conversations. He couldn't keep track of her lies anymore.

He shouldn't have come to the shop at all. He should have just left Mohon's and gone for a walk by the riverside instead – another of his favourites when he didn't feel like the long hike to Central Park. He used to sit on a bench and watch men throw down their fishing lines, the bicyclists and female joggers whizz by, admire their fine form, think of the time when he could run like that. Sometimes in summer he went early in the morning and saw the sun rise over the East River. He sat for an hour, perhaps two, watching the sky change colours. Behind him, only one avenue over, traffic would begin to build. The delivery vans would clog the roads. But there would be nothing obstructing his view, this shimmering gold water.

Usha was making plans with Jaya now. She was talking about meals at five-star hotels and whom she would visit first. 'We'll see you that afternoon of course, but after that, maybe we should call on his brother, then Mithun. And that evening, you and Amar and the children will come by for dinner. But it can't be too late. He'll be tired you see.' Mr Munshi was quite sure he heard something about a trip to Orissa. She might as well have been making plans for the Riviera.

When his wife was away, it was different. Then it was she who called, at exactly nine. If he didn't answer for some reason, she'd ask, 'Where were you? Why weren't you here? Did you have your tea? Are you feeling all right?' He didn't mind. He actually liked hearing her voice from a distance. After four decades of marriage, the idea of her was soothing.

Buku Sarkar grew up in Calcutta. She lived in New York for 14 years where she completed her BA at New School's Riggio Honors Writing Program, worked in publishing, ran a distribution agency and started a non-profit to encourage reading and recycling in the city. She is working on a collection of stories set on a stretch of Lexington Avenue in New York. Buku currently lives in Norwich with her dog and cat.

Alice Slater

In The Frame

Extract from a work in progress

Poppy and Dylan were playing Scrabble on the living room floor. Ignatius was asleep on the settee.

'Who's winning?' I asked as I unwound my scarf and shrugged out of my bulky winter coat.

'We're not keeping score,' Poppy said.

'Then what's the point?'

'She refused to play if we kept score,' Dylan said, frowning over his little rack of plastic letters.

They had cans of lager and a bottle of bourbon, so I popped open a beer and settled on the settee, nestling my face into the cat's warm belly. The mouth of the can emitted a golfball of foam. I hoovered it up with monkey-lips. The cat made a disgruntled 'brrrr' sound but permitted my presence all the same.

'I've got a great one,' Dylan said, clapping his hands together.

Poppy chewed gum and yawned. 'Just put it down then.'

'It's your turn though.'

She rolled her eyes and plonked three tiles in a crooked line onto the board.

'Nair? What does nair mean?' he asked.

'Isn't that a brand of hair removal cream?' I said, re-emerging from my feline pillow. 'You can't have that. It's not a word.'

'It's a word, isn't it?' Poppy snapped. 'You can say it with your mouth, can't you?'

'Another condition of play,' Dylan said, laying six tiles across the board, spelling out *quibble* with a flourish. 'We have to be flexible with the rules.'

Poppy took a long draught of lager. 'Can we stop now? This is literally the most bored I've ever been in my entire life.'

Dylan shook the bag of tiles, like a money bag. 'We've still got about half the tiles left.'

She gave him a withering look and started to light the dusty tea lights spread across the coffee table. He scooped the letters back into their green sack, then cracked open a fresh can of Kronenbourg.

'To Prometheus,' he said, and we all clinked tins. The candle flames flickered: a dozen miniature reflections were framed by his glasses.

'What's that?' Poppy asked, lighting a cigarette from one of the tea lights.

'Someone to whom you owe a lot of gratitude,' Dylan said.

'God, you're a drag.'

'I think we've got a mouse,' he said.

'On the tenth floor?' I replied. 'Don't be so ridiculous.'

'The washing powder box has been chewed,' he said. 'Unless Iggy has a penchant for nibbling cardboard, we have a mouse.'

'Eurgh,' Poppy sneered. 'I can only assume it hitch-hiked with you from your shithole house.'

'Iggy will catch it, won't you boy?' I patted the cat on the rump.

'That cat is barely capable of catching fleas,' Dylan said. 'I'll get a trap tomorrow. A humane one. Promise.'

*

'You're listening to *Nashville Skyline*,' Dylan said.

'Yes,' I said, from under the heavy duvet. He switched the light on. I blinked. The living room was still festooned with Edward Landeau's stuff. A life reduced to labelled boxes.

I stretched to switch the light off.

'Look, it's been weeks, Haze. Don't you think it's time we sorted out these boxes?'

'Maybe tomorrow,' I said.

Poppy came skidding into the living room. 'Oh, thank God you're back.'

'What? What's wrong?' he said.

'We caught the mouse,' she explained.

'*You* caught the mouse,' I said.

'The trap caught the mouse,' she said.

'*Your* trap caught the mouse.'

'Hazel.' She switched off the CD player and tugged at the duvet. 'We can't share our house with vermin. It's bad enough sharing with the ghost of Edward who's-its.'

I shrugged myself free, and followed them onto our cracked and weatherworn balcony. The rain had finally stopped. Ivy had overtaken the concrete back wall, and curled squid-like around the railing.

'Oh,' I said, dropping to a squat in front of the glue-trap. 'Poor little thing.'

'We should hit it with a brick,' Poppy said. It flayed and thrashed about, its feet immobilized, its tiny skeleton completely visible, ribs and miniature shoulder blades jutting through the cream fur.

'You're a *vegetarian*,' Dylan argued. 'I'm sure we can soak its feet in something, to unstick them from the glue.'

'It's white,' I said.

'No shit, Sherlock,' Poppy said. 'Maybe we could pop him in the freezer?'

'That means it's domesticated.'

'What?'

'It was somebody's pet,' I said.

We watched the squeaking mouse for a few minutes, arguing over the best course of action, before its tongue got stuck to the so-called 'humane' sticky pad. As it attempted to wrench itself free, gore spilt onto the glue, leaving a tiny red strip of tongue behind. Poppy screamed, covering her face with her hands, whilst Dylan stood in the kitchen nook and ran tap water into a mop bucket lined with dirt.

'Just hit it! Hit it with a brick!' she shrieked.

'I thought it was odd. Mice on the tenth floor,' Dylan said, returning with the bucket.

'Just *kill* it,' Poppy wailed.

'We should call it Poppy,' I muttered.

'What the fuck have I done now?'

'We'd probably do well by not getting too attached,' Dylan replied, dropping the frantic mouse into the bucket. Threads of blood marbled the water.

'Maybe you should've hit it with a brick,' I said. 'It will take a few minutes to drown. It's cruel.'

'No,' he said. 'Little lungs.'

Alice Slater studied creative writing at MMU Cheshire. Her work has appeared in the *Muse* anthology, the 6x6 Project and on Insanity Radio, London. She was shortlisted for the Bridport Prize in 2010. She is currently working on her first novel, a book about missing persons set in the liminal land of Crewe

Charlotte Stretch

Weightless

An extract from a novel

' … So he turns up, yeah, in a brand new Maserati. I mean, can you believe it?' Lucy swung around in her chair to see my reaction. 'I checked afterwards, and they cost, like, a hundred grand.'

I closed my eyes and pressed my fingers against my temples. Almost as soon as I'd woken up that day, my head had begun to throb with pain that wouldn't go away. And, to make it even worse, I'd had to put up with Lucy prattling on all morning. I reached for the packet of aspirin in my drawer.

'*Julia*,' Lucy nagged. I realised I'd missed the last thing she'd said. 'Don't you think that's true?' she asked.

'What?'

'That he's just trying to buy my affection. God, were you even *listening* to me?'

I swallowed two pills dry. 'Sorry,' I said. 'I was thinking about something else.'

She arched her eyebrows. 'Really? Anything interesting?'

'No. I mean, it's nothing.'

'I bet it's not.' She dropped her voice to a loud whisper. 'Are you hungover?'

'What?'

'The aspirin.'

'Oh. That. No. I've just got a headache, that's all.'

She laughed. 'Yeah, right. So you weren't out on the pull last night?'

I stared at her. 'No,' I said, insulted. 'I wasn't.'

She narrowed her eyes for a moment, sizing me up, then shook her head. 'Whatever,' she said. 'So anyway, you agree with me, right? About this guy?'

I sighed. 'Are you asking me whether I think someone would spend a hundred thousand pounds, on a car, for a date? OK. My answer is no.'

She pouted. 'Well, I don't know. He might have done. He's a hedge fund manager, remember? This is like *pocket money* to them. He was probably thinking of getting one anyway and decided to buy it in time for yesterday evening. Honestly, you should have seen how much he was showing off with it. It's like he really, *really* wanted to impress me.'

'Well, I guess if you're not going to see him again then it doesn't really matter,' I said bluntly.

'What?'

'You said he's trying to buy your affection. So I assume you won't be seeing him again.'

She frowned in irritation. 'I didn't say he *definitely* was. Just that he might be. And he turned out to be really generous, actually. He paid for all my cocktails in the bar. The bill was over a hundred and fifty.' There was a new boastful tone to her voice.

'How do you know that?'

'He left his credit card receipt behind. So I looked at it.'

'Ah. I see.'

I heard the door of Paul's office click open. He came out, clutching a sheaf of papers in one hand, and looked straight at me with a broad smile.

'Ah, Julia,' he said. He perched on the edge of my desk. 'How's things? Getting on OK?'

'Yes, thanks.'

'Marvellous,' he said, still beaming. 'I'm sorry I haven't been in the office much for your first couple of weeks – I've had to keep popping in and out.'

'That's OK,' I said. 'It's been quiet.'

'Which is good when you're new to the place, right? And what about Lucy – I expect she's been showing you all the ropes when I'm not here?'

I glanced over at Lucy, whose brow was furrowed as she stared at her computer, a look of deep concentration fixed on her face.

'Yeah,' I said, turning back to Paul. 'She's been great.'

'Jolly good, jolly good.' He flicked his blazer sleeve back with his free hand to inspect his watch. 'Well, listen, I was thinking – are you free for lunch tomorrow? There's a very nice Italian place in town. How does that sound?'

'Tomorrow? I … Sure. That'd be great.'

'Lovely. It's just a little chat, really, to see how you're coming along.'

'OK.'

'Great stuff.' He got up from my desk. 'Don't forget. And Lucy – make sure you finish that contract by this afternoon. I have to send it out before five.'

She flashed him a smile. 'No problem.'

As soon as Paul went back into his office, Lucy leaned back in her chair. 'Jeez,' she said. 'I wonder what *that's* about.'

'What do you mean?'

'Paul asking you out for lunch. No offence, but I'd be worried if I were you.'

I swallowed. 'I don't know what you mean. He said he just wanted to see how my work was going.'

'I know he *said* that. But – well, *I* didn't get that when I started here. Nor did anybody else. Paul usually just calls people into his office and says they're doing fine. So there must be a reason he wants to talk to you.' She picked up a pile of papers from a tray on her desk and began to sort through them.

I chewed my lip. 'He's been away a lot,' I reasoned. 'He probably just wants to know what I'm doing when he's out of the office.'

'I doubt it. He knows everything that goes on around here.' She looked up at me and smiled. It was obviously intended to be a reassuring gesture, but it came from someone who had no idea what a reassuring gesture looked like. 'Whatever,' she trilled. 'I'm sure it's fine. You've only been here a few weeks. They can't sack you yet.'

'Thanks.'

'Seriously,' said Lucy, flicking her hair as she turned back to her screen. 'I wouldn't worry about it.'

'I'm not worried,' I said.

*

That evening, I stayed at my desk for a long time after Lucy and everyone else had left for the obligatory after-work drinks at the pub. I liked being in the office by myself. The building had a calm, quiet atmosphere that wasn't there during the day. It felt especially soothing after an entire day of Lucy's ceaseless babble.

Her desk had been left a mess, as usual. Pens, old staples and paperclips were scattered across untidy piles of paper, which covered every inch of the surface. There was no one there to hear or see me, but I still held my breath as I pulled one of her drawers open, very slowly. Four loose cereal bars; a phone charger; some makeup; a magazine. The same one she'd been reading earlier. I pushed aside everything else in the drawer to look at it.

Promises of sex and diet tips were splashed across the cover, the letters jumping out at me in lurid colours. Retrieving the magazine, I laid it down on my desk and began flicking through the thick, glossy pages. All the girls in the photographs looked beautiful: slender, radiant, flashing huge grins. I stopped at one picture of a thin brunette posing with a handsome man, her skinny arms wrapped around his tanned, bulky frame. Her head was thrown back in giggling ecstasy. She looked a bit like me.

I slipped the magazine inside my bag. It was time to go home.

As soon as I stepped outside, I felt a bitter chill slapping against my skin. Raising the collar of my thin coat, I walked faster and concentrated on the warmth of my bedroom.

A few minutes away from the house, I turned my head to cross the road and caught sight of someone sitting by themselves on a bench, no more than twenty feet away. A lone middle-aged woman, shrouded in a heavy coat and scarf, at the edge of a neglected patch of park ground. She was sitting bolt upright, one hand crossed against her chest. The other held a lit cigarette in the air. My eyes were compelled towards this strange figure for several moments before I realised, with a shock, that it was my landlady.

For a second, I simply stared at her. We had been living in the same house for nearly a month, but I had never seen Clare smoke before. What was she doing here? Is this where she went when she disappeared from the house for hours at a time? I pulled my collar up as I approached the bench, shivering. In her thick coat, Clare didn't seem to feel the cold. She didn't seem to be feeling anything, in fact. Her face, always so careful not to give anything away, was blanker than I'd ever seen it. She just stared ahead while her cigarette burned all by itself.

'Clare.' She didn't look at me as I sat down next to her. 'Clare,' I repeated. 'Are you OK?'

Her face turned towards mine, and she stared at me with dead, empty eyes. I hesitated, not sure if I should rest a reassuring hand on her shoulder. No. Too awkward. I tucked my hands inside my lap, rubbing them together for warmth.

'Hey,' I said softly. 'Are you OK?'

She blinked then, as if she was suddenly seeing me for the first time. Her lips pursed together before she spoke.

'Yes,' she said, in a voice that didn't sound like hers. 'I'm fine.'

'Are you sure? How come you're sitting out here all by yourself? Aren't you cold?'

'I'm fine. I told you. I just needed to get some fresh air.'

Her cigarette, still propped between her fingers, had nearly burned all the way down. She didn't even seem to notice that it was there. I wondered if she had smoked any of it.

We sat there for a few more seconds, until I couldn't bear the awkwardness any longer. I stood up.

'Listen,' I said. 'If you're absolutely sure you're all right ... '

'Yes!' she snapped. 'I already said I was. You don't need to keep asking me.'

'I'm sorry.' In spite of the cold, my face flushed. I bit my lip. 'I think I'm going to go back to the house now.'

She closed her eyes. 'Fine.'

'OK. Well ... I'll see you later, I guess.' I hesitated. 'Bye, Clare.'

I waited for her to say goodbye, but she didn't say anything. So I turned around and carried on walking home.

Charlotte Stretch was born in 1983 and grew up in Surrey. She studied English at the University of Warwick before spending three years as a legal sub-editor. She is currently working on her first novel: a ghost story, narrated by a recovering anorexic, that explores themes of motherhood and family.

Catriona Ward

The Glass Resounding

The following is an extract from a novel, a ghost story told in three first person narratives over the course of the late 19th and early 20th centuries. This section takes place in 1889.

I laid eyes on Alonso first. It was the day we laid knife to our cadavers. I recall it as if it were a tintype; the image is curiously inert, and dull coloured – perhaps because the memory lives in my intellect and understanding, rather than in my eyes.

There was no horror in that room. I was put in mind of York Minster, which I have seen once, and the cool effigies that lie there in the sanctified air. The corpses were washed and bound in cheesecloth. There was little in the waxy figures before us to revolt. They lay like brides, each on their bier, the white forms barred by a little sunshine that strayed through the high windows of that echoing hall.

It was a pioneer scheme, this allocation of one corpse to two students, counter to the accepted practice of lecturing from a platform, where we would stand around, craning our necks to see the quick and tiny movements of the knife. Instead, we were to keep this person, or these remnants of a person, for our very own, throughout Anatomy. Month by month we would open them, piece by piece, organ by organ. The scheme was the cause of great outrage in the newspapers, for there was then need for thirty corpses, not just one. I had read an article in the *Penny Illustrated* only the day before, telling how it would lead to an increase in grave robbing, that the bread would be torn from the mouths of hardworking men and their families as a result. How the one would affect the other remains a puzzle to me. Burke lay in a glass case in the Edinburgh medical college, reduced to flayed skin and skeleton, Hare was forty years underground; both long gone. These cadavers had been obtained by means which were perfectly proper and according to the letter of the Anatomy Act. But this made no odds to the general populace, who wrestled with the conundrum: doctors must be trained, but corpses *must* be buried.

We set to work, with the stentorian tones of the lecturer in our ears. We began on a leg. The shape, the roundness of the calf, the muscles preserved so tight and solid beneath the waxy skin. There is a peculiar pleasure to it. The knife went in; the dermis, and layers of muscle were revealed like a flower, petal by petal. There were such colours and shapes. I had not known. The muscle is a rich purpled red, encased in marbled flesh, which is the colour of a baked salmon. The sinews and tendons have a white and yellowish tinge. The component parts lie tight together in symmetry, as if designed by a master craftsman, bound and run through by the lacework of corded vessels. The graceful long saphenous vein, from which other veins branch like winter trees against the sky. The rippling surface of the gastrocnemius muscle.

I was bemused by the vomiting and the distress that was engendered in my fellows. Unclothed, these forms retained their modesty. They were not awesome, but simply the carcase of man, sloughed away when need for it was done. The corpses were strongly preserved in formaldehyde; their flesh bore little relation to that of a living being. There could be no kinship to oneself – I could not think – *there but for grace go I* – or – *one day I shall lie thus*. Perhaps, upon reflection, I should have thought these things. Perhaps I was too sure and young truly to understand the condition of these cold figures, which submitted to the outrage of our knives.

Afterwards we sought the Lamb and Flag like hounds. Those of our party were seized by a hilarity commensurate to their previous unease. These young men now shed their fear and talked loud and brave. Scorning the hypocrisy of tippling by half measures, quaffing porter and blue ruin, faces grew rosier, lips wetter, eyes brighter. Their memories of the blood and the bones and the delicate layers of subcutaneous flesh were transmuted and the company waxed lewd.

Presently we were increased by a party fresh released from their lectures at Pall Mall East, and there was further frantic passage to and fro between tables and bar. We were busy as rats in an old cheese loft. One Irish gentleman whose name I cannot now summon besought me in plaintive accents to lay bets for the bareknuckle fight in the yard later.

'For we have not enough entries, Danforth, for a book, and it is Murchison, you know, fighting against a Black, and the Black sure enough to win.'

I demurred. I have always abhorred and avoided all forms of gaming and violence; here the two were promised to be mingled in fine anarchy. My finances were somewhat straitened, anyhow. I could not have paid my shot. He would not relent, however, and shouted that not for nothing were we drinking in the 'Buckets of Blood' (for this was the casual name given to the establishment in which we sat) and were to see a little fisticuffs and make up a book, so that he may buy ribbons for his little sister *after all*! The mention of ribbons had the happy effect of diverting his talk and he began then to describe a house he had patronised the night before, with entertainments I would not believe, he assured me. He began to tell me a tale of a pair of little twins, as perfect as they could be, who would do something with a live snake, but as he went on, his urgency and his consonants would not ally together with the drink he had taken. His breath carried an odour of halibut, and sorrow. It was no trouble to get away, now, and presently I saw him collapsed on a settle, mouth open, forelock damp, sleeping like a babe.

As the sun fell, the light grew orange and straightened its beams through the casements. Without, ladies had begun to show themselves in the street, fresh from their couches, to take the cool, yellow evening air. Through the rippled glass there could be seen gloved hands and the pale silk of dresses. They did not linger by the house, and I cannot blame them for it. I imagine our hullaballoo could be heard perfectly well as far as Covent Garden.

One man alone I observed, who sat quiet and played with a penny on the rim of his glass, producing a tuneful sound, never loud enough to attract notice but so that the gathering became accustomed to the gentle noise running beneath the babble. I thought he had arrived with the others only that minute, then I thought I had seen him in the hall that morning.

This man was sallow, and vast. His hair stood up at the back of his neck like the ruff of a bird. His linen was ragged at the collars and stained with ink, which also covered his hands like a blemish. He hunched in the settle chair like a crouching beast, his great oblong face hung above the table, hollow eyes fixed on his task, which he performed with movements that were precise, and small. The great fingers manipulated the penny with a dexterity that confounded the eye, ran supple and light around the dirty rim. An image, a memory perhaps, arose unbidden to the surface of my mind: of him holding a knife, face solemn in the dim air.

No, I thought he had not, after all, been with us this morning, for I was sure I would have noted him. I shook my head to clear it of the heavy punch fumes and moved closer, under the cover of the shrieks. One bright spark had donned the tavern madam's bonnet and was discoursing in a theatrical voice on her 'pullets' and 'spiced wares' which were for sale. This was enough distraction for the company, who rocked with laughter.

As I moved my stool, I was clumsy and made a business of it. The wooden legs screeched on the flags. The penny man lifted his eye to mine. Within the caverns of his face, it was that of a blackbird, bright, and deep like a glimpse of the bottom of a well. His finger sent the coin singing once more around the rim.

'They hear it,' he said, 'but they do not mark it. It is a constant. They have accustomed themselves. But if I increase the pitch so,' he poured more ale into the glass and it sang out higher, 'and so on, eventually the glass will shatter. That, they will note. There will be a great fussing with cloths and restitution and a new glass, as if it were a surprise. But the warning has been sounding.' He sang the glass again, 'All along. Do you understand?'

'I do not, I confess.' I was held by the lights that moved in his eyes.

'It is so that death sits beside us every day, until it is forced upon our notice. Until the vessel breaks open and life flows out we must be blind and deaf to its presence, or we could not conduct our carnival as we do.'

He gestured at the youth who entertained the company. That

individual was now bright red. The bonnet lay askew over one eye, and he had begun a series of high kicks, as the Parisian dancing girls do. The penny man regarded this with kindness, but absently, as if it were an effort by a child to imagine a giraffe when they have not seen one.

He went on, 'But there are some who choose to listen to the song of mortality which underlies it, lies beneath everything. The long note beneath the cacophony. For those who can hear death, whistling always, underneath; who do not fear him, but see his part in the music.' He grasped my arm as if in sympathy, 'For them it is a vocation of the loneliest, and the highest order.'

We looked on one another. The finger turned and the glass whistled its distress. The pitch soared and enclosed us in its sphere.

'It will break,' I said.

'Ah. Not it,' he said. 'Not yet.'

I offered him my hand then and told him my name.

Catriona Ward was born in Washington DC and grew up in Kenya, Madagascar, Yemen and Morocco. She studied English Literature at Oxford University, where she was a scholar. For the last three years she has worked as writer and researcher for a human rights foundation.

Anna Wood

Rise Up Singing

You do get hot summers in Bolton and we had one that year, for weeks on end as I remember it although it may just have been a fortnight or so. This was a Friday so we had double English that afternoon with Mr Howard. Lisa and Claire had both taken a full tab, but Janey and I had only had half each.

'Who or what do you think is causing the friction here between Jane and Elizabeth?' asked Mr Howard. His hair was aglow and the walls pulsed gently. Lisa put up her hand but then pulled it down slowly and shot it up in the air again. She did this a few times, mesmerised. Claire sat to Lisa's left, giggled and swooned.

'Lisa,' said Mr Howard. An acknowledgement of her pumping arm.

'Mr Rochester,' said Lisa, beaming. It was impossible to know whether she had forgotten Mr Howard's name or whether she was simply talking about the wrong book.

Claire was stroking her copy of *Pride and Prejudice* and crying. 'There's no need for any of this,' she said, her voice quiet and bleak.

'Sir,' my voice came out too loud. 'I'm taking Claire out of class. She's not well.' But then the bell went, and class was over anyway. I had no idea where those 80 minutes had gone and suspected the clock or the school or the bell of some mean trickery.

Janey and I started walking into town, down long empty Deane Road, away from our classes and classmates. My ears were slipping gently and endlessly towards my neck while Janey kept tapping her arm with her forefinger to see if it was solid. The pavement smelled dusty in the sun, the terraced houses were red and warm. We waved at cars, who occasionally honked back at us, and we sang. 'Say it's only a paper moon,' at a passing Volvo Estate, 'Hanging over a cardboard sea,' at an XR2i. We'd been playing my parents' Ella Fitzgerald CD for weeks, all sophisticated.

It was so hot that we directed our feet to the shady side of the street, and even then we felt we ought to twist our T-shirts at the front and tuck them over into the neckline, our 16-year-old midriffs in the open air and our 32A bras showing. A tee-kini!

Before we got as far as town, there was Toys R Us, all solid and primary colours by the roundabout. 'We'll go and play,' I told Janey. 'We won't steal anything.' Inside we found a quiet corner with mounds of plush, squidgy dogs and rabbits and cats. I plunged my arm into a pile of white puppies, up to my elbow, and felt the softness and warmth. I compared my skin, the holes and tiny criss-crosses and hairs, to the gleaming, lifeless fabric of the toys. 'Everything that is good smells and moves,' I told Janey, hugging her, smelling her.

We steered well clear of the little circling helicopters on the way out and ran the last five minutes into town. When we reached the square, panting, I tried to work out where my lungs were. 'Higher than you probably think,' Janey informed me. 'Way up here,' she patted my shoulder, more or less. 'Remember you've got to have room for your liver and your stomach too. They're all protected behind your ribs.' I was besotted by the earnest, teacherly tone in Janey's voice, but I knew better than to think for too long about my internal organs after taking acid.

We sat on the steps in front of the town hall, in the full sun, watching Bolton. We tracked cute boys across the square, gazed all giddy when Neil Curtains and Hot Colin, sitting on a bench just outside Superdrug with their legs sprawling, pulled off their T-shirts, stretched their arms along the back of the seat and let their heads loll back, eyes closed to the light. Their necks were muscly, lumpy invitations, curving and throbbing.

'Should we eat soon?' Janey asked.

'I've got a spliff at home.' I had most of a bag left in my sock drawer, although my house was a bus ride away. 'How can we get there?' For a moment the journey seemed unthinkable, and then we forgot that it was.

We walked part of the way, through the park, making a list of the worst haircuts in history and which character from *EastEnders*, if we really had to, we would shag.

'Roly!' I shouted, to make Janey laugh, and she did. When we saw the 617 coming, we ran and caught it, the day still bright but not warm enough for our silly bellies. We pulled our T-shirts back down, winked at a small grey-haired woman, felt rude, smiled.

My parents weren't home. We went up to my room, stopping in the kitchen to get chocolate digestives from the cupboard and to lift Clementine, our ginger cat, from the sofa. 'Who's got better coloured hair?' Janey asked, lying on my bed and tugging on her own copper hair, draping it over Clementine's head to give our cat a sort of toupee. Janey's hair used to change colour, quite dramatically and quite naturally – it was brighter in the summer and some kind of red forest universe in the winter.

'Can you still feel that trip, Janey?' Mine was almost gone.

'My arms feel stretchy,' she observed, extending an arm and contemplating its length, her fingers playing an invisible keyboard. 'But maybe they just *are* a bit stretchy. It's time for some alcohol anyway.'

So we got ready to go out with a bottle of Cointreau from downstairs sitting on my table next to the stereo and the moisturiser and the make-up. We took sticky sips and had quick showers and decided what to wear (Janey borrowed my white jeans again). It was a gentle excitement. We were in no hurry because the night was waiting for us.

We got off the bus a stop early, just outside the town centre, so we could go to the corner shop and each buy a flask of Pernod – £4.49, fits into the back pocket of your jeans and tastes good poured into a pint of blackcurrant for 50p behind the bar at Fifth Avenue.

We never did have that spliff at my house, so we decided to take another half tab each before we went in. 'Let's not get fucked,' Janey said. 'But let's get a bit fucked.'

The entrance to Fifth Avenue had two bouncers, and then you pushed through big silver doors into a dark room with low ceilings and lights, blue, red, green, yellow, jerking and swinging.

What do I remember? That night, or another night, I danced to Sylvester with a man I didn't fancy but who danced all fast and hips and fun. I kissed a man called James with long curly hair who was at least 25. Which was old. I told him it felt like a film-star kiss, which meant, 'Why didn't you put your tongue in my mouth?' Leanne was there with Briggsy and Briggsy's mate Clive. Clive talked a lot. He looked like a lizard, his eyes tick-tocked in their sockets and his skin was leather. While he talked, he sat on the floor in the back of the room. The fire extinguisher behind him whispered over his shoulder, making it difficult to concentrate on whatever he was saying. The toilets were busy and we were desperate so we peed in the sinks. No one minded. Then later I went to the toilet again with Leanne's little brother who had cocaine. I thought he might kiss me but we just took the drugs. Christine and Rhona from Canon Slade didn't talk to me. They never liked me or Janey but I don't remember why.

Then 'Let's go home,' Janey said, and we did. We left early so we could miss the cheesy last song and get chips in pitta over the road without having to queue.

The taxi place was quiet too. It was still warm and two drivers sat outside, smoking and watching the drunk people. 'Where you headed, girls?' I don't recall his face but the sight of his belly, just the pale hairy roll of it between his T-shirt and jeans, lodged in my brain.

'Markland Hill,' Janey told him. She was not entranced by the belly but was stroking the front of her face as if it was a cat. 'Just by The French Arms.'

'That whole street was bombed years ago love, in the war.' Not a glance to his mate, not a snigger, nothing. 'We can't take you there.'

Janey swung round, chin tucked down, and linked her arm into mine. She steered me away, taking short, fast strides. 'What's he on about? Wanker. He knows we're fucked.' She began to laugh, and I did too. We were singing again, 'Summertime!' Yelling really, at the stars and the chimneys. 'And the living is e-e-e-easy!' The thought of jumping fish made me itchy with pleasure. We were, I suppose, higher than the cotton. 'My daddy is quite well off,' I admitted to Janey. 'And my momma is well fit,' she said.

I started to cry when I remembered that this was the song my parents used to sing to me when I was very small. I felt lucky, I think, and guilty. I felt something, and I didn't want it to be nothing just because I'd had some drugs. Janey sat down next to me on the pavement. 'You're a good girl,' she told me, stroking my shoulders, squeezing me. 'We're good girls.'

For a minute I thought the growling was Janey, trying to make me laugh. I growled back, and she said, 'What are you growling at, dafthead?' Then, like slow-motion cartoons, we turned round to see a dog just behind us. Growling. He was just behind a fence, too, which was good news because he was a dog that looked like a furry muscle with teeth. The fence was tall.

'Dogs know when you're tripping,' whispered Janey. This is true, I thought. The dog knows. He was in a frenzy of growling and twitching now. He was headbutting the fence. Janey had a look of delighted horror.

'Just slowly walk away,' I told her. This was a serious situation requiring a serious voice. The dog stopped growling, watched us clinging together and shuffling down the pavement. Then we saw that the gate was wide open.

'Ha!' Hysterical air shot from Janey's mouth. 'Fence high,' she said to me. Whispered. 'Gate open.'

'Fence high,' I repeated. 'Gate open.' We swerved into the road, across to the other side, did not look back, and ran. The dog was probably inches from us, perhaps jumping at our backs. We kept on up the street and home.

My mum and dad had left the hall light on for us. I unlocked the back door, enjoying the fit of the key in the lock, thinking about metal and wood and hinges and the weight of things. Janey was thinking about the dog. 'Fence high,' she repeated. 'Gate open. Fucking hell.'

'Fence high,' I said, putting my hands up in the air to demonstrate. 'Gate open,' I stretched my arms wide and pulled a silly face of panic.

'Shhhh!' Janey told me, giggling, and we went in. Kettle and sofa and telly. Janey would sleep in the spare room same as usual. I had a pair of pyjamas that I didn't wear anymore because I thought of them as Janey's pyjamas.

While I made us Horlicks, Janey sat on the kitchen floor in front of the open fridge. She scooped houmous from a tub into her mouth, using two fingers. I whispered to myself, 'Fence high. Gate open.' In the next room, *The Twilight Zone* was just starting.

Then my dad appeared at the kitchen door in a T-shirt and boxer shorts. He blinked and shrank a little from the light. I was still lost in the magic of how kettles know when to turn themselves off. Janey was humming to herself, although there was no tune as such.

'Did you two have a good night?'

'Yes, Mr Marshall!' sang Janey. She straightened her back and waved the tub of houmous as if it was proof of all the fun we'd had.

'Yes, it was fab,' I said, teaspoon clinking on the mug.

'Good stuff. Sleep tight, then.' And he stood for a couple of seconds in the doorway, his head tilted to one side, smiling.

Anna Wood is finishing her collection of stories based on the nightlives of women in Manchester and London over the past 20 years. She grew up in Bolton, studied English at the University of Sussex and worked as a copy editor in London before moving to Norfolk for the creative writing MA.

Wu Xianlin

Novel Extract

Below is an extract from a novel in progress, which retells one of the best-loved myths in the Chinese canon: Wang Zhaojun, who lived in the Han Dynasty roughly 2000 years ago, was a maid-in-waiting before the emperor married her to the king of the Huns as a peace offering. Throughout history she has been used as a yardstick of female virtues. This novel gives her a modern voice and re-examines her life not only as a historical figure but also as a cultural image in today's world.

Sometimes she presses her ears against the wall, to listen to the giggling or the muffled, rhythmic groaning on the other side. She has met her neighbours, of course, the new ones as well as the old. They always come and go, depending on looks or age. But the noises stay the same.

She has good ears, she knows. Only she knows this. Good eyes and mouths are harder to hide, and therefore mean more trouble. But good ears are a secret that she can indulge in. Not that she intends to be deceptive. Not at all. She simply needs to know where she stands, or where she would stand in her own absence.

Imagine all the stench and squalor!

Do you know they eat their prisoners and slaves? I'd rather die first ...

He will jolly her up. At least she now has something real between her legs.

Of late she has been spending a lot of time listening, behind wooden screens and closed doors. Broken sentences, missing names, conspiratorial simpers. Dabs of colour she has used to build a picture of him, or rather, of her future in light of him. It is to these rumours that she listens most avidly, her body tense with the thrill. That Hun, they will say. Not ever his name, or his title. For them it is accurate. She is marrying a species, an inferior life form that thrives on plundering and raw meat. Why name a rat?

She refers to him as the Hun, too, when there is an expectant audience. But this is because she can't decide her feelings. She is angry with him for her confusion, and with herself for allowing it.

When they swarm to her door, gift-bearing and chests puffed up with spurious envies and congratulations, she subtracts herself, lets her mind wander. Some offer her dainty little souvenirs of sisterhood: an embroidered silk fan or purse. What do they expect her to do with a fan in the freezing steppe? Maybe it is their idea of a joke. Or she can probably use it to drive away the flies and mosquitoes and all sorts of vermin that are sure to abound in that barbaric land. She will not throw them away, yet.

More than once she has wondered if they made these presents themselves, cursing her under their breath for the trouble. They might have sent some eunuchs to make the purchase in the West Market. From some poor malnourished girl with chapped hands and grubby nails. Such a thing is entirely possible. Or is it the East Market that sells these gewgaws? It has been so long, and she has lost her bearings. She is being mean and cynical, she realises. But it is reassuring to know that she can still afford it. What they really want is to see her dissolving in a pool of tears, like a snowman in the sun. She will not give them that satisfaction.

There are girls who are genuinely sorry to see her go, but she avoids them as well. Compassionate sighs are more ruinous. Look at the bright side, they say sadly, their painted brows knotted up in a frown, their mouths trembling. This annoys her. *You will be waited on hand and foot. Such luxury! Think of that!* She doesn't think she will, not without disgruntled silence or contemptuous glances at least. But there is no point in contradicting them. They mean well, she tells herself.

The eunuchs are her only hope. Especially the younger ones, with their guileless smiles and loose lips. She will drag one by the sleeve behind a bush, pry him open with a handful of coins. Being in close quarters with them always fills her with unease. They have an untouchable air about them, the eunuchs. A perennial odour of urine encircling them like a cage. Animals stake out their territories in the same way, she thinks.

That Hun is quite a wise man for a barbarian – one informs her, jingling the coins – he has the brain to see that battling against us mighty Han will do him no good. He is a traitor to his own people – says another – who has sworn allegiance to the Emperor and drunk blood from a hollowed-out human head. There is talk of internecine strife, the death of a brother. In her mind she has expected thin sinister lips, bulgy eyes. Forehead riddled with blue veins.

She tries to summon up all the ghosts she has created for him, willing them not to inhabit the man sitting on the dais. Slow yet sure-footed, she moves forward. The music engulfs her like water.

Come closer, the Hun says uncertainly. Words tumbling out of his mouth like dice.

She stops in front of a flight of marble steps. At her eye level there is a low jade table, maroon brocade draped over it. Someone's fingers have embroidered a dragon on it, expertly, with meticulous stitches. It is an art she has taken pains to master herself. She resents the display of effort. This is what I will always remember, she tells herself. But why such lugubrious thoughts? Surely there is silk and thread in the barbarian land. Maybe there will be fur-embroidery. She will be able to occupy her time.

Two men are sitting on the dais. The Emperor is barricaded right behind the table, dressed in a black satin robe with a dragon pattern on it, she knows without looking. Over to the side, in the subordinate seat, is a pair of furry knees. His knees. She pictures them knobbed, pachydermous, legs bowed from too much horse-riding. What does he expect to see on her face? Joy? Or is it shyness? Flushed cheeks, rigid jaws, a bashful fluttering of eyelids. She can bring that into effect. She has seen others at work. Or perhaps it is fear that he desires, the tremulous tension in the muscles. There is nothing like a hint of terror to encourage conquest.

The music stops. A sudden heaviness falls on her body, as if she was coming out of a river.

The Hun scrambles to his feet clumsily, stretching his legs as if unfamiliar with the movement. She watches him lurching, limping a few steps, knocking over a bronze drinking vessel. A trail of spilled liquid. She wonders, only briefly, who will wipe it clean later, all fours on the ground. He is not used to sitting on his heels, she realises with dismay.

Steadying himself, he brushes down his baggy fur robe apologetically, as if caught naked, descends the stairs.

She kneels. A sharp crack from her defiant bones. She lowers her head, hoping no one has noticed. The guardians have taught her etiquette in a sympathetic undertone. They have sat her down, almost solicitously, cradled her hands with their coarse palms as if to protect her. As if her hands were the only thing that needed protection. They rubbed her fingers while they talked, until her skin turned red. They explained the pains and unmentionables that would follow the wedding, thrust a scroll of inscribed bamboo slips under her nose. Isn't this for the wedding night? she asked. Well, better to be prepared earlier in your case. They said this with the self-satisfied air of fortune tellers, their eyes on her, maliciously curious. They anticipated that she would writhe, wail, tear her hair and make a scene. They would be disappointed if she didn't.

He picks her up, his hands strong as clamps. She tries not to recoil. She wonders if there will be red imprints left on her arms, the seal of ownership, like those on cattle or horses. She can almost feel her skin burning in his grip, under layers of silk.

Still not knowing how she will adjust her face, she lifts her head slowly. It is an act, the deliberate slowness, the lethargic grace. She has acquired it unconsciously, the way one picks up the local accent. It is not an unhandsome face, she thinks, but wrinkled and darkly tanned. Through the grizzled thicket of whisker she can see his mouth cracking into a smile. A row of ragged, yellow teeth.

Without releasing her arms, the Hun turns to his entourage. Voices brush past her like foliage. A volley of foreign words. What are they saying? She feels a sudden surge of anxiety. Comments about her inadequacies perhaps. The flatness of her chest, for instance. Or maybe it's not her flaws that they are talking about. Maybe it's her strangeness, her sheltered, delicate skin, which is equally dispiriting. She catches a glimpse of a patch of pale skin amidst the nest of greying hair. Something contracts in the pit of her stomach, as if she had just swallowed a mouthful of icy water.

Then, abruptly, they fall silent. They all turn to look at her. She wants to say something. She feels it is called for. Some words she has learned, her tongue groping desperately as if to pick at scraps of food caught between her teeth.

Chenli Gutu Chanyu, she murmurs. Heaven. Son. Vast. Son of the vast Heaven. Or is it son chosen by the Heaven? The word is slippery, skittering away from her mouth like a knocked-out tooth.

The man laughs. A gust of stale, alcohol-reeking breath unfurls from his mouth. She can feel the softness of her own skin in his grasp, his thumb rubbing hers reassuringly. She will need to wash her hands later, she thinks. She watches him swivelling around, waddling back up the steps. With an ostentatious reluctance, he lowers his haunches onto his heels.

All the Huns join in the laughter as if on cue. So do the huddle of Han officials on the other side of her, though with less vigour. These are her people, she thinks. A shot of something sour goes up her nose.

The eunuch is still hovering at the entrance, a dark figure against a background of fading light. She imagines him watching her standing alone in a valley of men, surrounded by echoes not of her own voice.

She clenches her fists. A dribble of blood snakes down her fingers, vanishes into the dark red sea of her robe.

Wu Xianlin was born in Shanghai where, after completing an MA in English Literature, she wrote her first novel, *Glass Eyeballs*. She came to England in 2009 to study writing and is currently working on her second novel.

Life Writing

Introduction by **Kathryn Hughes** *and* **Richard Holmes**

Thea Abbott

Desmond Avery

Nicoletta Demetriou

Francesca Kletz

Wendy Knowles

Juliet Miller

Maureen Phillips

Elizabeth Michelle Ruddick

As far as Life Writing at UEA goes, the class of '11 have produced a bumper crop of contributions. There are eight pieces here, each one fizzing with style, energy and invention. For if one thing is clear, it is that the definition of 'life writing' is more generous than ever. Forget about cradle-to-grave narrative, what we have here are elegant interventions, playful riffs, shimmering meditations on a whole series of lives, from the artist Richard Long to the writer Colette by way of an elderly North American couple living in a mobile home (just don't call it a trailer).

Thea Abbott gives us a rich description of intellectual semi-bohemian life in Soho just after the Great War, centring on the studio of stained glass artist Ethel Kibblewhite. A hundred years later, the sculptor Richard Long proves to be a far more elusive subject for Juliet Miller, who describes how she almost failed to recognise her subject when she arranged to meet him at the Arts Club. Desmond Avery reminds us of that clever, gentle publisher-baronet, Sir Richard Rees, who midwived the work of two very different authors of the mid-twentieth century, George Orwell and Simone Weil. Francesa Kletz, meanwhile, reveals in a sharp, witty essay that she never gets to the point of working out who she wants to write about, since the only person who really interests her is herself.

Elsewhere in this collection, Nicoletta Demetriou uses food – the memory of it then, the taste of it now – as a way of exploring her own family history. Elizabeth Michelle Ruddick reconstructs an imaginary meeting between Colette, one of Europe's most celebrated writers of the Modernist era, and Violette Leduc, 'the most famous unknown author in France'. Wendy Knowles produces a generous yet unsentimental assessment of Robert Skidelsky's career-skewing decision to write a biography of the Fascist leader, Oswald Mosley. Finally Maureen Phillips gives us a sad, funny account of going to see her elderly parents hunkered down in their pride and joy – a mobile home that comes complete with its own showroom accessories, including a ball of knitting. Truly, all life is here.

KH

Now celebrating its tenth year, the remarkable UEA Life Writing MA has pioneered a unique blend of disciplined seminars and highly individual research projects. It is renowned for its enthusiastic atmosphere and supportive style, and has already fostered a number of published non-fiction writers. I hope to see it go on from strength to strength.

RH

Thea Abbott

The Two Sisters

The two sisters could hardly have been more different, one adventurous, athletic, confident, the other, according to family accounts, retiring, self-effacing and just downright unlucky. Yet it was Ethel, the unlucky one, born in 1873, who survived and Dora, two years younger, who died tragically young.

They were born in the St Pancras area of London, and the 1881 census shows them living at 30 Robert Street, near Regent's Park. Their father, Thomas Figgis Curtis, was a stained glass artist, and in 1883 he took over the firm of his employer, Curtis Ward and Hughes. In their heyday the company had employed 100 painters, glaziers, lead workers and designers producing windows for churches and civic buildings all over the country. They operated from a building at 67 Frith Street, on the corner of Soho Square, which had once been the Venetian Embassy in London. It was an imposing building with a great central spiral staircase leading from the street entrance level down to the basement and up to the three floors above. The business operated from the ground floor and the basement and yard, while the family lived on the upper floors – above the shop as it were. Towards the end of the 19th century, Thomas bought the 17th century Walnut Tree House in Rustington in Sussex, and his family moved down to the country with Thomas visiting at weekends.

There are wonderful descriptions of Frith Street and Walnut Tree House in the memoirs of Ethel's son, Peter Kibblewhite, and though they are based on his own childhood memories, life might not have been so very different when Ethel and Dora were growing up. He describes Walnut Tree House as an Edwardian idyll: constant summers, jam cooling on the steps outside the kitchen, pigs and hens in the outhouses, a gardener called Frank who taught him to make snares for rabbits and rats, fishing for sticklebacks with his sister Diana, and a pony and trap for trips to the nearest railway station at Arundel from which his grandfather travelled to and from London. But this is a boy's memory of exploration and play, and I think the girls' lives will have been more like his description of his sister's 'work' at Walnut Tree House, where he tells us that,

> while I spent most of my time outdoors in the garden, my sister Diana worked with Grannie at cooking and sewing, at both of which crafts she became very skilled. Grannie was a great seamstress and embroiderer. She made a beautiful set of curtains of wool embroidery to an old English design and all the sofa and chair covers and chintz curtains for the bedrooms. All my grandfather's clothes – even to his jackets and cloaks and trousers came from her stitching. Socks, sweaters and gloves were knitted by Grannie … and very comfortable they were to wear.

There must, though, have been more to the girls' lives than just rural domesticity because they both attended the Slade School of Fine Art. They are registered as entering together in 1892 – the year when the great Henry Tonks began his teaching there. They had already been studying drawing in London with Frederick Brown and their entry to the school must have been influenced by his opinion of their work.

Dora became a successful illustrator of children's books, and designed fabrics for Tootal Broadhurst and Lee. She was also a traveller and an adventurer, often away from home for extended periods. Members of the family remember her as 'a stormy petrel', because wherever she went 'trouble seemed to break out'. She visited China as a member of a missionary group, and was caught up in the Boxer Rebellion (1898 - 1900), fleeing a thousand miles and more down the coast in an open railway truck just in front of the advancing revolutionaries. She was in the Balkans in 1912 when the Balkan war broke out, and only narrowly escaped to England. Later, in 1914 she travelled to Siberia with an expedition led by Maria Antonina Czaplikca, to study the people of the Yenesei River. The party comprised Maria herself, Dora as official artist, Maud Havilland – an ornithologist, and the only man – Henry Hall, an American anthropologist. In her book about the expedition Maud Havilland gives this description of Dora:

> Then there was Miss Dora Curtis, an artist. A better comrade for such a journey it would be impossible to find. Always in good spirits, and keen for either work or play, always the very soul of good nature and kindness, she was the life of the party, and later on contributed much to its material as well as to its mental well-being, as one who has had the good fortune to taste her cookery can testify.

The return journey to Britain was mistimed. Maud and Dora were ice-bound in the White Sea, above the Arctic Circle, and by the time they reached Scandinavia in 1915, they found that the Great War had begun. On arriving home in England Dora's immediate reaction was to join the Scottish Women's Ambulance Service. She was posted to France as a driver, later becoming personal driver to General Maugin as he pursued the retreating Germans. She was awarded the Croix de Guerre for her bravery! After the war she returned home for a while and then in 1919 she went on holiday to the Canary Islands. She was a strong and confident swimmer, and no one knows exactly what happened, but she was found drowned with a fractured skull in a rocky pool on a lonely part of the coast. The family view was that she must have dived into the pool and hit her head on a rock, but there were no witnesses.

Ethel, the older sister, who was known by family and friends as Dolly, was a talented water colourist – her paintings are delicate and beautiful. But when the market for stained glass declined, and business became more difficult for Curtis Ward and Hughes, Ethel was drafted in to work by gaslight in the evenings painting windows (she already had a job as a proofreader and editor at the Oxford Press). Her son Peter recalls her as a gentle soul who always got the worst of arguments with her younger sister, especially as their mother always backed Dora. In his memoir he writes that in 1900, with her 'characteristic bad luck, she had married a man five years younger than herself who turned out to have an uncontrollable temper.' Gilbert Kibblewhite was the second son of Ebeneezer Job Kibblewhite, a successful journalist. He was the black sheep of his family and never settled to any job. His father bought a smallholding at Storrington in Sussex, installed him as manager, and he and Ethel were married on 30th April 1900. A year later, their son Curtis Peter was born in London, probably while Ethel was staying with her parents to escape Gilbert's violence. She must have returned to her husband though, because the 1901 census records the family living at Scrag Oak Farm House in Wadhurst and Gilbert is listed as 'Farmer/employer'. Two years later there was a second child, this time a daughter, Edith Elinor Diana Chloe. By now the marriage was impossible for Ethel, and she was afraid for her children. There are family stories of Gilbert driving his horses so hard that he terrified everyone. Once he shot a horse dead in front of Ethel and the children. After that, fearing for her life, she decided to leave for good. She packed up her belongings and the two children and went back to live with her parents at Walnut Tree House. Peter's memoir tells us what happened next:

> Not long after our arrival at Rustington, I was woken early one night to hear an altercation at the front door of the house. Grannie and Aunt Dora detested Gilbert, and Aunt Dora, who despite her domineering behaviour towards my mother, was not slow to take up the cudgels on her behalf ... was to be heard refusing to admit him to the house. Eventually he went away. A few days later I was woken by our Nanny, Frances, with the astounding news, 'The Studio's burnt down.'

Peter is quite clear that his father was responsible. His grandfather's eight beehives were destroyed and he describes a 'pitiful line of charred timber and dead bees.' His grandfather 'usually the mildest of men, egged on by my mother and Aunt Dora, threatened legal action against Gilbert,' whose father arranged for him to leave for a new life in Australia. Ethel never talked about her marriage – it was merely referred to in the family as 'a terrible thing'. She and Gilbert were divorced twelve years later when he came back to England as a private in the Australian army during the First World War.

After her separation from Gilbert, Ethel lived in Frith Street and worked as a designer for the Royal School of Needlework in South Kensington. Her two children, Peter and Diana, spent most of their time at Walnut Tree House with their grandmother. In 1908 or 1909 Ethel met the poet and philosopher T. E. Hulme, they became good friends and she was probably his mistress. One of Hulme's biographers suggests that she had a 'horror of sex', not perhaps an unreasonable response to her terrible marriage, but most of their friends seem to have thought of them as a 'married' couple. By this time the Frith Street house was already something of a feature in London cultural life. Hulme kept a room there with his books and wrote there every day. He and Ethel held regular Tuesday salon meetings in the great first floor drawing-room with its magnificent chandeliers, where friends and fellow intellectuals met.

These included Wyndham Lewis, Ezra Pound, Henri Gaudier Brzeska, Jacob Epstein, Ford Maddox Ford and, on one or two memorable occasions, Walter Sickert. Hulme and Ethel spent hours playing *Go* (the Japanese war-game) compulsively – and their games were said often to end in heated argument. When, in 1911, Hulme's paper on Henri Bergson 'A Personal Impression of Bergson' was published in *The Westminster Gazette* it appeared under the pseudonym T. K. White, a play on Ethel's married name – Kibblewhite. There are accounts which suggest that Hulme's publications of Bergson's writings were actually made from Ethel's translations.

In parallel with this intellectual London life there was a completely different atmosphere in the country at Walnut Tree House, where Hulme and Ethel joined the two children Peter and Diana at weekends and in the summer. Pictures show a barefoot Hulme, who was a big man, rampaging in the garden with the children. Both Hulme's biographers, Robert Ferguson and A. R. Jones, repeat a story that Hulme promised to marry Diana as soon as she was old enough because she was such a good cook and made his favourite steamed syrup pudding so well.

Hulme was a notorious womaniser and had numerous sexual encounters with 'the shop-girl class', which Ethel seems to have ignored.

But her 'usual bad luck' continued and he developed a relationship with another painter, Kate Lechmere, and promised to marry her after the war ended. The couple's friends were divided into two factions, those who supported Hulme's decision and those who felt he was treating Ethel and her family very badly after such a long and close relationship. He claimed that he could never have married Ethel because of his strongly traditional feelings on divorce but there is no sign that he had made that position clear to Ethel. Hulme died in battle in 1917 before any marriage could take place. Ethel dealt quietly with his literary estate and his other affairs. No one knows what became of the bulk of his letters and unpublished writings, though Epstein suggests in a letter to a friend that they might have been burnt by Ethel. She did keep a pair of Hulme's boots though, and a few years before her own death she ceremoniously handed them on to her nephew Martin Kibblewhite (Peter's son). He wore them for several years before they finally turned up their toes in Sweden in 1955.

Ethel herself lived on peacefully in Sussex with her Siamese cats, gardening and reading and caring for her two children and her grandchildren, until her death in 1947. Who knows what Dora's life might have been had she lived so long?

Thea Abbott took her first degree with the Open University before settling in Norwich. The UEA Life Writing MA has provided two happy years and the luxury of writing for pleasure and perhaps, one day, for profit.

Desmond Avery

Rich and Strange: Sir Richard Rees, Editor, 1900-1970

If Richard Rees thought he had won immortality for himself by being George Orwell's best friend and publishing nine books, he was wrong. As far as I know, I am his last hope, and this will be the longest and best researched piece ever to be published on his life. His sister, Lady Rosemary Du Croz, gets a page in the *Dictionary of National Biography*, mainly because she flew her own aeroplane, but he gets nothing. Old editions of *Who Was Who* contain a paragraph on him, he makes brief appearances as a minor character in Orwell biographies, is occasionally mentioned in the small body of literature in English on Simone Weil, and, apart from his own books, all long out of print, that's about it.

Being keen on Orwell and Weil myself, I got curious about this fellow enthusiast, and eventually found 28 boxes of his papers in the Special Collections of University College, London. With their help, I can offer the following account of his life and works.

He was born in Oxford on 4 April 1900 and christened Richard Lodowick Edward Montague. His father, Sir John Rees (1854-1922), had been a five-language translator and administrator in the Indian Civil Service, a director of 13 companies (mainly tea, mining and railways) and then a Conservative MP for Nottingham, knighted in 1919. His mother was a sister of Lord Dormer, from an ancient Catholic family, but Richard was brought up mainly agnostic. He went to school at Eton, where he was not a scholar and did not know Orwell, being three years older than him, and then read history at Trinity College, Cambridge. He came into the 'Sir', denoting second baronet, at the age of 22, when his father died.

His inheritance enabled him to live for the rest of his life on an unearned income – something that always rather bothered him as his political convictions were, like Orwell's, mainly socialist.

After a brief Foreign Office job in Berlin in 1922 and a job at Cambridge University Press in 1923, he worked in London for the Workers' Educational Association from 1925 to 1927. The next episode is accounted for by chance in an undated draft letter he wrote in later life to a Mrs Lawson in which he says: 'I have personally visited each of the three famous modern psychologists, Freud, Jung and Adler … I was *completely* out of action for four years, from my 26th to 30th year, suffering from depression, lack of confidence and inability to face life.' In 1930 he became 'angel and co-editor' (Sonia Orwell's expression) of *The Adelphi*, a literary journal started by John Middleton Murry in 1923 to propagate his own beliefs, which seem to have rescued Rees from his doubts and fears.

George Orwell was also in trouble in 1930, as a destitute would-be author, and Rees took an encouraging interest in his work, gave him books to review, published articles by him, and lent him money. In 1937, inspired by Orwell, Rees left *The Adelphi* for Spain, where he became an ambulance driver, after which he did refugee work for Spanish exiles. In the Second World War, he served as a gunner in the Royal Naval Volunteer Reserve, and then helped to look after Orwell as he struggled to complete *Nineteen Eighty-Four* while succumbing to tuberculosis.

After Orwell's death in 1950 and Murry's in 1957, Rees turned most of his attention to Simone Weil, the French philosopher, factory worker and mystic who died of tuberculosis in Ashford, Kent, in 1943 at the age of 34. He had never met her, as he was at sea when she was in London with the Free French, but was inspired by her writings which had begun to appear in French soon after the war. He became friends with her brother in New York and her mother in Paris, translated her essays, letters and notebooks, and wrote a short biography of her with her family's help. He also wrote and published a memoir on Orwell and three books of essays, and edited two collections of essays by Murry. Rees left unpublished a novel, a further book of essays, and more translations of Simone Weil's writings. A prolific writer, editor and translator in his sixties, he died suddenly in hospital in London, after an operation, on the morning of 24 July 1970.

At the time of Rees's death, Murry's widow praised him for his 'genius for friendship'. Others recalled his kindness and conscientiousness. One called him 'too good for this world'. Rees never married, and his last close relative as far as I know was his sister Rosemary who died in 1994 at the age of 93. He wrote of himself that he had no children, but his agent's assistant at Peters, Fraser and Dunlop said their file on him mentioned a daughter called Pamela Ann Watling, with no details or contact data. The only Pamela Watling I succeeded in finding denied convincingly all possibility of being Rees's daughter.

The photograph of Rees in D. J. Taylor's *Orwell: The Life* shows a worried-looking balding man with wide-open haunted eyes, a furrowed brow and several days' growth of grey stubble. He looks rough, like Don Quixote down and out in La Mancha. Taylor's book has this troubled face next to a cheerful one of Eric Blair at the age of about 20 looking like Sancho Panza – chubby, with twinkling eyes and a silk cravat. Bernard Crick mentions 'Sir Richard' frequently in his *Orwell: A Life*, but provides no picture except verbally as a rather ridiculous high-minded aristocrat and the model for Ravelston in *Keep the Aspidistra Flying*. In that novel Orwell gives Ravelston a voluptuous girlfriend to sleep with, but no evidence has come to light so far of any such item in Rees's life. Gordon Bowker numbers him among Orwell's friends who were 'either gay or inclined that way,' which is safe to say but hard to spell out. Rees noted that he destroyed 'a lot of letters and documents bearing on my sexual and other obsessions in the past.' About some of the papers I have not yet seen, the archive keeper says 'there may be Data Protection issues.'

Rees wrote his first book at the age of 57: *Brave Men; a study of D. H. Lawrence & Simone Weil*. It is a striking subject but a difficult one, and hopes for enlightenment are dampened by his opening words: 'If a thing is worth doing, it is worth doing badly, as G. K. Chesterton said' – surely not the right way to start, but, sadly, it sets the tone for his more ambitious writings. By comparing the thoughts of his two 'brave men' on love, death, suffering, transcendence and related matters, he argues that 'it would be impossible to choose two better guides than D. H. Lawrence and Simone Weil through the purgatory of the twentieth century.' Now that we have got through that century, it would be very hard to argue that we would have done better if we had been guided by them. Rees's insightful memoir on Orwell was almost certainly the most read of the five books he wrote. *For Love or Money* which preceded it and *A Theory of My Time* which followed were a mixture of memoir, random philosophy and literary criticism.

He had a great deal to get off his chest in his old age, but it never seems quite to come together in a powerful piece of writing. This is intriguing in its contrast to Orwell, who had many of the same opinions, was probably just as confused in many areas, was as uneasy about his own poverty as Rees was about his own wealth, and yet, from about 1936 onwards, wrote with resonant strength consistently. Rees frequently sounds like a gibbering ghost from my parents' generation, whereas Orwell's voice continues to ring true.

Rees's work on editing and translating Simone Weil was excellent, however. In 1958 he wrote to André Weil, her brother, for permission to publish a selection of her essays in English. André, who was then a professor of mathematics at the Institute for Advanced Studies in Princeton, welcomed the proposal but explained that his mother would have to agree to it too:

> Unfortunately (as I once explained to Sir Herbert [Read]), she has engaged into a never-ending series of law-suits against me, and we only communicate through our lawyers. It should only be a formality easily fulfilled (even though my mother's state of mind, being what it is, one can't even be quite sure about that); but it is an indispensable one.'

Selma Weil, the mother, was a strong character, and so was André. In the emotional discussions about what to do with Simone's chaotic mass of writings after her death, they had disagreed irreparably, both considering themselves to be the keepers of the flame but with incompatible ideas of how to go about it. André favoured a systematic publishing programme for her complete works according to a thorough academic classification and editing of them, whereas Selma favoured a trade-oriented approach, supported by Albert Camus at Gallimard. She was financing the lawsuits against her son out of royalties for her daughter's works, while her husband stood helplessly by. Rees nevertheless became a good friend in the Paris and the New York camps alike, deploying his niceness and his prestige as a titled English man of letters with flair. By that time he had had plenty of practice in this branch of literary diplomacy with Sonia Orwell, his famously flighty co-executor of Orwell's estate.

There are some quite different aspects of his life and character to take into account as well, such as his 'genius for friendship'. Frieda Lawrence, who thought T. S. Eliot had 'no blood, no guts, no, marrow, no flesh,' did not see Rees like that at all. A letter she wrote him from her ranch in New Mexico, warmly invited him to stay:

> If ever you feel you want to refresh your soul & forget about the rotten part of humanity come here – you can have a log cabin and you would like Angelino, he is so natural – one lives with the sun & the desert & the cowboys are Mexicans, my bread is so good & the vegetables & the horses have just eaten a lot of corn, and the coyotes one gorgeous moonlit night tore a young sheep to pieces & a weasel has bitten my two kittens to death – that is also nature sweet and pure & don't let's forget it!!

'Alas, I never went,' says Rees, but it hints at wilder dimensions of love and friendship in his life than those we have seen so far.

His unpublished novel, called *The Wrong Name*, opens with a quotation from Simone Weil: 'What we are talking about is the very thing your soul desires, at this moment in your present state. Only you give it the wrong name.' It is partly in the form of a diary kept by a respectable male academic who secretly fell obsessively in love with men and eventually died, I think by suicide. When I read it before, I noticed mainly how unconvincing the whole thing was – and the occasional cigarette burns on the old foolscap pages. Secker & Warburg rejected it firmly, and I'm sure they were right. Then while I was writing this account, a diary Rees kept during his naval service came to hand, and it recorded strikingly similar experiences as his own.

'Obviously, no full explanation of a man is ever possible,' he wrote towards the end of his book about George Orwell, and it is even more obvious of himself than of his friend. Part of him seemed keen to tell his whole story, while another part remained anxious to keep it hidden. Dear Richard, I hope this very short account will help you to continue to do both.

Desmond Avery is the author of *Beyond Power: Simone Weil and the Notion of Authority* (Rowman & Littlefield, 2008) and *Lee Jong-wook: a Career in Health and Politics* (World Health Organization, 2012).

Nicoletta Demetriou

Cooking and Eating the Past: Reflections on Food and Memories

I grew up in a place where everything – and I mean *absolutely* everything, from welcoming a new baby into the world to saying goodbye to someone going into the other world – is marked by some sort of eating ritual. What's more, I was born into a family where cooking was neither only a necessity nor simply a pastime, and where it most certainly wasn't a chore. Cooking – or, more accurately, feeding us – was, and remains, my mum's *raison d'être*, what defines her as a loving and nurturing mother. Still, I hadn't quite grasped the effect that cooking and eating has had for me in reconstructing my past, its centrality to my very being, until very recently. Last year, as I began to write my short pieces for biography class, week in, week out, I noticed that food, cooking, and eating kept creeping into my narrative again and again. When I was asked to write my first ever memory, it was to do with food:

> I am four years old. My mother has gone to her driving lesson, and I'm left in the care of my grandmother. She is 75 years old, dressed in a black robe and black headscarf in the village fashion, can neither read nor write, and only speaks her village's dialect. It's mid-morning, so she prepares breakfast for both of us. In the middle of her small room is a green gas heater, and on its surface she toasts sliced bread and black olives. That's our breakfast: toasted white bread with margarine, and toasted black, salty olives. On her cooker my grandmother prepares a cup of Turkish coffee for her,

sweetened with two sugars. When the coffee is ready, she puts it in her little coffee cup, and carefully spills a little in the saucer. She hands the saucer to me, so that I, too, can have a sip of coffee, just like her.[1]

Months later, in autobiography class, I was asked to reconstruct an early memory. Food again:

My two older sisters are arguing in the kitchen. I don't like it. My mum has just brought a shopping bag with crisps and juice. My sisters keep arguing, I can't remember what about. I take a packet of crisps – a Mr Chips red packet, salt flavour – and some juice – Pip juice, grape flavour, in a small white plastic cup with purple letters, sealed with aluminium foil. The juice is nice, but I remember the flavour of the plastic rather than that of the juice. I go out in the garden, and sit alone in a quiet corner, so that I can enjoy my crisps and juice without my sisters shouting. It's an autumn morning, and although it's a bit cold, the sun is shining. At some point the shouting stops, and my mum realises that I'm no longer in the kitchen. She rushes out shouting my name. She sees me sitting in my corner in the garden, enjoying my snack without a care in the world. She goes back in and gets the camera, and captures the moment for eternity. And so here I am, twenty-six years later still sitting in the garden in my blue velvet dress, smiling while I enjoy my Mr Chips crisps and my Pip grape juice.[2]

A few weeks after that I was asked to write down my first food memory. Well, where shall I begin? It seems that most of my childhood memories are connected to food, cooking, eating, to kitchen sounds and smells. I remember my grandmother frying meat marinated in sweet red

1 Writing exercise, Biography module; 8 November 2009.

2 Writing exercise, Autobiography module; 8 February 2010.

wine, or manically hitting an octopus in our yard to break its fibres before cooking it; I remember those huge Christmas lunches (I have 33 first cousins alone) with the endless array of dishes arranged on every available space in the kitchen; I remember my mum cooking early in the morning, and me waking up to the smell of cinnamon and mint coming from the kitchen; I remember the *flaounes*, the Cypriot Easter cakes, hot out of the oven every year on Good Saturday morning, and all women in my neighbourhood proudly displaying *their* cakes to their neighbours; I remember these same women's blackened fingers in early summer, when they were all peeling fresh, soft walnuts to boil in water over days and preserve in thick syrup for that wonderful *glyko tou koutaliou* ('spoon sweet'); I remember deadly hot afternoons sipping ice-cold rose water with sugar, into which floated a piece of *mahallepi*, a rice flour paste; and I remember *kollyfa*, boiled wheat served with pomegranate, sesame seeds, blanched almonds and raisins, brought to us by our neighbours late on Saturday afternoons, right before Vespers, when the neighbourhood folk remembered their dead. Where shall I begin?

* * *

The most famous recipe in *The Alice B. Toklas Cookbook* is, without doubt, that of 'the food of Paradise' – the hashish fudge, 'which anyone could whip up on a rainy day'.[3] Yet of all of Toklas's recipes, the one that confirmed itself as truly enduring is that of the book itself: the cookbook-slash-memoir has proven to be an inimitable hit. The word 'cookbook' may well appear on the book's cover, however Toklas's book is much less that and much more a memoir. The stories she writes about travelling around France with Gertrude Stein, having lunch or dinner with all manner of people at all kinds of places, and tasting or cooking all sorts of delicacies (or peculiarities, depending on one's palatal preferences) are the real heart of her narrative. And that's what's kept the book on bookshop shelves for the last fifty-something years, not the recipes. Even

---

3 **Alice B. Toklas**, *The Alice B. Toklas Cookbook* (London: Serif, 2004; first published by Michael Joseph, 1954), p. 259. In the *Cookbook* the word 'hashish' is spelt as 'haschich'.

if Toklas's recipes might have once tempted cooks and food lovers to try them out in their kitchens, I can't imagine anyone today injecting a cognac-and-orange marinade into 'a simple leg of mutton' with a surgical syringe for a week and then serving it with '2 tablespoons of the blood of a hare',[4] nor cooking '2 dozen plucked larks',[5] nor roasting the 'saddle of [a] young boar'.[6] And frankly, I can't imagine anyone now buying this black-and-white book for its recipes, when there are hundreds of cookbooks with mouthwatering colour photos out there, which require no 'murder' to be committed in the kitchen before the cooking can begin.[7] In *The Alice B. Toklas Cookbook* the recipes are there to complete the picture, not to create it.

> Partly, I suppose, [the book] was written as an escape from the narrow diet and monotony of illness, and I daresay nostalgia for old days and old ways and for remembered health and enjoyment lent special lustre to dishes and menus barred from an invalid table, but hovering dream-like in invalid memory.[8]

Reading Toklas's 'mingling of recipe and reminiscence',[9] I wonder how much of it was written as nostalgia not 'for old days and old ways', but for her beloved Gertrude, the time they spent together and the trips they took, and as a way to bring her back. 'Gertrude Stein said ... Gertrude Stein requested ... I told Gertrude Stein ... Gertrude Stein and I ... ' If the friends Toklas reminisces about are the spices of her book, Gertrude Stein is undoubtedly its salt and pepper.

---

4 Ibid., p. 33.

5 Ibid., p. 246.

6 Ibid., p. 61.

7 I'm referring to Toklas's chapter 'Murder in the kitchen', describing how she (or her servants) had to kill several animals before cooking them. Toklas, *Cookbook*, pp. 35-46.

8 Toklas, *Cookbook*, p. xi.

9 Ibid., p. 61.

* * *

Much has been said and written on the nurturing side of cooking, on how feeding people is a way to show our care and love. But if cooking is connected to nurturing, then eating is certainly connected to sharing: sharing time, sharing a meal, a kitchen, our life. Nothing could help us reconstruct our past more successfully than thinking about time shared with others around a table, seeing, smelling and tasting food.

Molly Wizenberg was thinking something along these lines when she decided to set up her food blog, Orangette, shortly after her father had died of cancer. She was trying to make sense of her past, enjoy her present, and bring her loved ones closer to her.

> When I walk into my kitchen today, I am not alone. Whether we know it or not, none of us is. We bring fathers and mothers and kitchen tables, and every meal we have ever eaten. Food is never just food. It's also a way of getting at something else: who we are, who we have been, and who we want to be.[10]

Every time I open a bottle of sweet red wine to pour over some pork, my dead grandmother of twenty years comes back from her grave. And every time I bake my Cypriot Easter cakes in London, no matter how grey and rainy outside, the smell of cheese and mint and raisins turns the inside of my flat into a glorious Mediterranean spring. If I want to bring my friends from Thessaloniki a little bit closer, nothing does it better than if I fry their favourite potatoes with crushed coriander seeds. And never can I bake a banana cake or knead dough and not remember my gloomy year in Vienna, where the lack of flatmates, a boyfriend and a TV taught me that the best way to pass a lonely night is to bake to your heart's content.

---

10 **Molly Wizenberg**, *A Homemade Life: Stories and Recipes from my Kitchen Table* (New York: Simon and Schuster, 2009), p. 2.

Cooking and Eating the Past: Reflections on Food and Memories

As a teenager, what seemed to me as my mum's obsession with cooking drove me mad. Why couldn't she just leave the kitchen, sit down and relax like the rest of us? It took me many years to realise that that was *her* way of showing her love day in, day out, and I'm only now beginning to appreciate that her marking every important and not-so-important occasion in our family life with a shared meal is what now helps me put the memories of my past together.

Similarly, the memory of my grandmother is so vivid in me, despite the fact that I shared with her only the first twelve years of my life, partly because of what she cooked for me, what she fed me, and how her kitchen smelled. And that's how she got to be the protagonist of my first food memory:

> Sweet red wine is inextricably linked to my grandmother and hence my childhood. No meat could be fried if it was not previously soaked in sweet red wine. As I cook in my London flat, annoyed that I can't get sweet red wine here, I remember my grandmother's fried pork chops that were almost caramelised when fried, *kolokasi*, a type of sweet potato that changed its colour from white to brown after being soaked in sweet wine with meat, little cubes of pork again soaked in wine and cooked with dried coriander seeds ... [11]

If cooking defined my mother and grandmother, what defined me for many years – as the youngest and most rebellious daughter – was my crusade to prove that I was *not* my mother. I managed to trick almost everyone – even myself – but a great big smiling realisation was lurking about, waiting to laugh at my face, serving me a dish of cold revenge. 'Hey you', it finally asked, 'how do *you* show your loved ones that you love them? How do *you* mark important occasions that you want them to remember for years and years to come?' 'Well', I stumbled, 'I ... cook.'

---

11 Writing exercise, Autobiography module; 1 March 2010.

References

Toklas, Alice B., *The Alice B. Toklas Cookbook* (London: Serif, 2004; first published by Michael Joseph, 1954).
Wizenberg, Molly, *A Homemade Life: Stories and Recipes from my Kitchen Table* (New York: Simon and Schuster, 2009).

Nicoletta Demetriou was born and raised in Nicosia, Cyprus. Before coming to the UK, she lived and studied in Thessaloniki (Greece) and Vienna. She holds a PhD in Ethnomusicology from SOAS, University of London, and has recently been elected Alistair Horne Visiting Fellow at St. Antony's College, Oxford, for 2011-12.

Cooking and Eating the Past: Reflections on Food and Memories

Francesca Kletz

Artistic Empathy

'I am not the empathiser I had always hoped to be!' I cry out, woeful, desperate, my negligee saturated in lipstick, ink stains and bile. Surely part of being an aspiring, or a fledgling biographer, is that I can relate to people; I can sniff out a story from another's life and turn it from history into prose. Oh yes, it's all so glorious, sitting, dreaming for hours about how I will one day be crowned an established writer, how people will flock to me with their stories, with ancient manuscripts in tow and secret estates to which millions have attempted to gain access. I will be the one they all want, to turn them from people into stories, to be enjoyed for hundreds of years.

So here lies my problem; I don't much care for other people.

It is so incredibly difficult to find another with whom you are fascinated enough to spend hours reading and writing about. I am envious to the point of exasperation in reading stories of other, actual biographers who have become obsessed with their subject. In honesty I do obsess, but it is an obsession which resides almost wholly in myself. As I sit in the bath restyling my mass of Ashkenazi hair, I think of all the other women who do the same and think that perhaps I ought to dig for people who are similar to me. Then, as if there was never another thought in my mind, my glance is redirected and I think how big and blue and close together my eyes look in the misty reflection of the tap.

My interests in life writing began when I was assigned a project on sculptress Camille Claudel. 'There is a novel about her life' was whispered to me as I left my classroom that afternoon; straight to

Amazon I went, browsing the pages for this text which I had no idea was about to kick-start the biographical cogs lying dormant in my head. As I read about the life (albeit a fictionalised version) of the mistress of Auguste Rodin, I fell in love. This woman was passionate and creative; she was marvellous to read about and even more wonderful to research. What's more, she reminded me of myself. Here I had found a kindred spirit, her childhood hopes that she would be a recognised artist, her dreams of perfect love and her paranoia that the bourgeoisie of nineteenth-century Paris would laugh at her legs, one shorter than the other. How I cried with compassion when I read about her ailment, for I too have a strange gait and have often ventured into London, desperately hoping that the scenesters won't notice the bizarre angle at which my right knee bends.

So there you have it, I absolutely can empathise. Yet, I am still at a loss for subject matter, a lack of another to relate to.

Perhaps my problem is with laziness rather than disinterest; I reflect on my backlog of failed attempts at hobbies and sports. Gaps in my repertoire where I had intended on taking music exams, delicately fading certificates for various stages of Ballet, a Tae Kwon Do uniform still stiff with starch and about four years between attempts at jogging. Days languidly snoozing on my mother's couch stuck with me and merely assisted me in all areas of procrastination and self-indulgence. I can't help but think of Camille's father finding her as a child playing in the mud, sculpting her family in perfect formation – an accomplished toddler.

I spent my Christmas holidays writing about my grandmothers and their cooking. I never met either woman but with my love of all things edible, all things Jewish and 'ahem' all things relatable to me, I just knew I would enjoy writing up my research. I adored discovering the lives of these two women, their routines, their clothes, their pastimes … their creativity and senses of humour and all the other wonderful attributes I had been searching for in my lineage; the reason I am who I am … this distracted and self-centred being. I felt I had at last been able to relate to my subjects and perhaps this was the perfect place to start – subjects within which I could see myself and therefore connect to their pains and habits and ideas. When feedback was ready for my perusal I was yet again to be shafted by my solipsism. Yes, it was a lovely essay ... oh! and those snippets of autobiography worked beautifully ... the best parts perhaps. My attempts at writing about others had once again fallen under my egotism and no veiling mass of curly hair or recipes for heirloom chicken soup could resuscitate them.

As I have worked my way through coursework, desperate to tap into an empathy which may one day render me publishable, the prospect of a new subject looms on me but only ever in the shape of my own gargantuan shadow. At this age Camille had already began her affair with Rodin, her influence had already chiselled its way into his marble and she had some essence of the love she always dreamed of. I can't even pick an essay topic.

Camille, so desperate to sculpt, stole her clay from the upturned streets of Paris, she lived through the revolution, never letting poverty and sickness turn her from her need to create. I can hardly distract myself from *Match of the Day* and I, with my knee bent anti-clockwise, have previously never taken an interest in sports.

I couldn't see a topic in anything we had read or discussed. I proposed to do those presentations that were based on subjects I knew I could throw myself into: cookbooks and books written about adventures in Scandinavia. Rather than the literary research and the deep dive into the subject's lives as my peers were doing, I spent my preparation times toasting crushed coriander seeds, peppercorns and almonds for Alice B Toklas's Hashish Fudge and scrolling through pages of blogs about Scandinavian street style and speaking to a Danish friend about Swedish marzipan buns. There was no room for any serious empathy in this round of study.

I reflected on autobiographical studies on Mary Wollstonecraft's adventures in the North, her travelogue of letters written to a man who no longer wanted her. How she had spoken so Romantically of Scandinavia gave me chills as I recalled my recent trip to Copenhagen and how I had felt enigmatic on my departure home, sure to return to this bizarre and breathtaking kingdom. With every chip on my new ring, adorned with the emblematic Daisy, I felt a pang of upset, as if the hard, conservative edges of English table tops were trying to disengage me from my love of the Danes and their wonderful customs ... and their stunning floral harem trousers. Learning about Mary's heartbreak, suicide attempts and instabilities whilst desperately trying to remain a respected advocate for women's rights was touching, but again my connection with her lay in my own life and any empathy lay in memories of my own past sadness. As I began constructing my fictional account of her upset I realised how strongly I was drawing on my own experiences of unrequited love and disappointment. I wrote about myself but masked my experience with Mary's and replaced the names of those I miss with Mary's dispersed lovers and long dead acquaintances.

I have found solace in cooking. I have found myself depending on Friday night dinners to fill my week with some routine and an accomplishable edible intention has overcome my need to complete my assignments. It is so simple for me to pick something to cook, if only I could think of a subject to whet my appetite in quite the same way, my writerly equivalent to saliva. I have even let cookery intervene with my essays. According to my account of Mary Wollstonecraft, she copied up recipes to soothe her spirit and regain sanity. I have become fixated with cookery books, I adore flicking through batter-encrusted pages and I am obsessed with tasting the outcome (of the recipe, not the encrusted page). Food memoirs are often bestsellers and I would enjoy basing my writing on some area of my consumption but I doubt my gluttony will be of any interest to a reader, or indeed a publisher.

Mary Wollstonecraft's writing began to adjust when she reached twenty-eight. Her publisher Joseph Johnson found her increasingly 'self-conscious style'[1] amusing and to me, her last published book *A Short Residence in Sweden* is the greatest display of her literary talent. Perhaps my writing will be increasingly less self-indulgent as I mature. Yet I can't help but think that Mary's Scandinavian travelogue is as close to self-indulgence as a writer can reach. The letters are written with an intention of guilting her disinterested lover back into her arms. Mary even threatens never to reunite him with their daughter. This is selfish writing at its best and perhaps it is her detachment from her previous texts which make *A Short Residence* such a great read; the reader is wholly

---

1 *Mary Wollstonecraft A Revolutionary Life*, **Janet Todd**, GB, Columbia University Press, 2000, p 120

Artistic Empathy

invited into Mary's heart, we know who she is.

My devotion to writing comes from an interest in the self. Being picky and stubborn about subject matter is imperative to the success of my work; I want to empathise with a few and I want to despise the rest. I consider my discernment a gift; it means that when I have made that rare connection with another, it will give my writing an extra ounce of passion. It is also important not to take your obsession too far. Let this be a lesson to those of you who have (like me) declared yourself the reincarnation of your adored subject; my heart practically dissolved when I read on about the great sculptress. Camille Claudel was sent to an asylum when she was thirty-nine, her affair with Rodin had been finished for years and she had few friends. Until she was carted off, she lived secluded in her atelier in Paris, surrounded by stray cats. She died thirty-nine years later in the institution, paranoid and abandoned by her family. She was buried in a communal grave in the grounds of the asylum and her funeral was attended only by a few of the nurses on duty. Needless to say, when I had finished my project on Camille I decided that there were in fact a hefty number of dissimilarities between us. However, the connection I had felt with her never ceases to be wonderful; that empathy I had had for her moved me and made me want to seek out others to whom I could also relate. For me, life writing is about finding the soul of another and, in doing so, discovering more about myself; even if that discovery leads to nightmares about asylums, moulded clay and a writer's annex filled with cats.

Francesca Kletz is a monumentally stylish, London-based, Ashkenazi Jew. She studied Art History in Canterbury and Amsterdam before road tripping around North America and Australia. She wants to write about food and is hoping to turn her dissertation – a biography of the pickled cucumber – into a book.

Wendy Knowles

Captive Scholar

'**M**ost scholars remain captive to their first adult piece of research', argued Robert Skidelsky. Out of his own doctoral thesis, published to acclaim in 1967 as *Politicians and the Slump: the Labour Government of 1929-31*, would grow his 1975 biography of the Fascist leader, Oswald Mosley and, later, his prize-winning biography of the economist, John Maynard Keynes.

In his biography of Mosley, Skidelsky described the role of the biographer as being not that of 'prosecutor' but 'somewhere between that of counsel for the defence and judge'. He argued that most of what had been written about Mosley in recent years had been from the prosecution point of view and that it was time to see him as a figure of history rather than demonology. His first encounter with Mosley had been in 1961, at the Oxford Union, where even the young Paul Foot, famously Marxist, had commented on the brilliance of Mosley's speech against the motion proposing that South Africa be expelled from the Commonwealth. 'My interest in him was born at that point,' the historian recorded. Perhaps he felt sympathetic towards the disgraced politician, because of his own outsider background. That theme of 'insiders' and 'outsiders' runs through much of his writing. The Skidelskys were Russian Jews who had escaped from Bolshevik Russia during the Russian Revolution. Although they escaped with a fortune, most of that money was lost in the stock market crash of 1929. They settled in Harbin in Northern China to run what was left of the family fortune, a coalmine, but this too was lost after the Communist takeover.

Outsiders again, the family came to Britain in 1947. For the Labour Party supporter (as he described himself in the biography) and friend of Oswald's son, Max, it had taken courage for Mosley to come to the Union and it had taken intelligence and brilliant oratory to 'gain a triumph in that stronghold of liberalism'. How was it that a man who possessed such gifts could have fallen so low? How could this once Tory politician, then prominent Labour politician of the 1920s, a man who had at one time seemed genuinely concerned with getting rid of unemployment and securing world peace, have become the infamous black-shirted monster of the 1930s? It was a question that captured the imagination of the independent-minded historian, who had a penchant for challenging conventional assumptions. The subject of much of his research over the next twelve years, Mosley would cast a shadow over his career.

In his thesis Skidelsky took the view that the British unemployment problem of the inter-war years could not have been effectively tackled within the framework of a political struggle between the Conservative and Labour parties, between Capitalism and Socialism. His joint 'heroes' were John Maynard Keynes, the adviser whose advice was rejected and Oswald Mosley, the Labour minister who resigned when his 'New Deal' for dealing with unemployment was turned down – two men, with big personalities, who wanted to cut through the restrictions of party politics. This was the scene that Skidelsky's biography of Mosley revisited. But when Skidelsky's account moved away from his thesis, he was on rather more dangerous ground. This was the next phase of Mosley's career, his fascist period and its most contentious elements: his encouragement of anti-Semitism and political violence, and his attitudes to Nazi Germany and the Second World War. Why, when Mosley had so much to lose, did he throw it all away? Was the decision to do so rational – was it the outcome of his thinking that the liberal economic system was doomed and that the existing elites lacked the will and mentality to create a new system to deal with the economic crisis in time? Or was it a decision rooted in temperament and outlook? Skidelsky took the view that it was a result of both. However, this did not explain why fascism provided the only answer. Many others had the same objectives as Mosley but did not become fascist. Skidelsky's academic critics were not slow to pass judgement.

Skidelsky's chosen role as sympathetic biographer was not the problem, argued Professor John Vincent in the *TLS*, while drawing his readers' attention to the co-operation that Oswald Mosley had given Skidelsky in the writing of the biography, and the fact that Mosley had thanked him for his assistance with his own autobiography, as a 'younger literary friend'. This collaboration does not 'impugn the author's delicately trailed liberal credentials' and was 'in line with the author's declaration that it was "time that the case for Mosley was made by the historian".' However it was the author's failure as a 'historian' in this 'indeed personal book' about which he was most critical. Searching for the 'liberal' hero who had lain undiscovered in Mosley, Skidelsky had come up with just about enough evidence to 'justify a long essay'. That alone was crushing enough but Professor Vernon Bogdanor, writing in *Encounter*, was equally critical. In attempting to understand a totalitarian leader, Skidelsky had fallen into the trap of 'special pleading', of omitting facts whose introduction would disturb the picture that was being painted. In Bogdanor's opinion, Mosley was 'the hero – a deeply flawed hero, but a hero none the less – of this biography'. More importantly, though, Skidelsky's emphasis on Mosley as a Keynesian radical had led to his failure to pass moral judgement on Mosley's fascist phase.

The liberal academic reaction to the biography is said to have resulted in Skidelsky being denied a professor's tenure at Johns Hopkins University in Washington. Worse was to follow. He believed that he had been effectively 'blackballed' by Oxford University, where he had been a student and a Nuffield Research Fellow. From 1976 to 1978 he took the job of Professor of History, Philosophy and European Studies at the Polytechnic of North London, an institution famous for being a hive of radical political activity, where Skidelsky felt 'like a fish out of water'. The post was not what he had hoped for. Significantly, he does not mention his time there on his website. It was not until Warwick University took a gamble on him and offered him a Professorship of International Studies in 1978 that Skidelsky came in from the cold. At Warwick he went on to publish his acclaimed three-volume biography of the economist, John Maynard Keynes, the other 'hero' of his first piece of research.

Was Skidelsky guilty as charged? After all, he had claimed that the role of biographer was not that of prosecutor. Answering his critics, he argued that in most biographies, although there would always be a tension between successful biography and successful history, the effort to understand and explain the motives of the subject was taken for granted. Only when the biographer's subject was a 'bad man' was it interpreted as special pleading. With hindsight he should have corrected more against this biographical bias but he suspected that he would still have been accused of undue sympathy. What his critics were really objecting to was his choice of subject.

Today Skidelsky's biography is seen as breaking the mould in attempting to debunk some of the Mosley myths. It sparked off a debate that continues still as to whether Mosley's fascism was a response to the events of the time or a product of his temperament and character. But it is Stephen Dorril's exhaustive biography, *Blackshirt*, published in 2006, that is now regarded by many historians as the last word on Mosley. The brilliant politician, who had apparently entranced everyone from the moment he was elected, had also, as Dorril points out, aroused suspicion in many. Beatrice Webb was not the only one who 'smelt a rat'. Hugh Dalton wrote, 'Mosley stinks of money and insincerity'. Stanley Baldwin called him a 'wrong 'un'. But the adjective that was most commonly used to describe him was 'arrogant'. Drawing on fresh archival sources and papers that were not available to Skidelsky, *Blackshirt* charts a much darker life of Oswald Mosley, 'Fascist'. Dorril reveals that Mosley lied persistently about his party's funding by Mussolini and Hitler. Imprisoned during the war under emergency regulations, Mosley and his wife Diana spent their time in prison reading and learning German. Neither of them ever showed any signs of remorse. Moreover, both refused to believe that they might ever have been wrong or to recognise that Fascism in Britain had failed abjectly. They were, however, Dorril tells us, keen to rehabilitate their own reputations in the eyes of the British Establishment and to conceal key areas of Mosley's political activities. In 1967, Diana Mosley informed Skidelsky's literary agent that there would be no conflict between Sir Oswald's autobiography – 'the opening of negotiations for peace with the British Establishment' – and 'the authorised biography that is being written by Mr. Skidelsky'. That word 'authorised' is crucial. Skidelsky's biography, with its focus on 'the central episode of your life – the period 1929-1931 – which is not only right, but also most favourable to you', would be the high point in Mosley's rehabilitation.

In his role as Mosley's authorised biographer, was Skidelsky bound to establish what sympathy he could with his subject and hunt out any redeeming feature? I do not think so. His job as an objective historian was to look at all the evidence, as Dorril does, and present a case for his readers to make up their own minds. But, as with most authorised biographers, there was an implicit contract, and one that Skidelsky referred to obliquely in 1988, citing his own personal golden rule for biographers: a refusal to write official biographies. Here is what Diana Mosley had to say in a letter to her sister Deborah Devonshire in 1975, soon after the biography was published:

> Robert says historians now are intimidated & one must not mention certain things. His great crime is that having ferreted out police reports of the thirties he found that most of the violence was Jews attacking Kit's [Mosley's] people in dark lanes etc. Sorry darling I won't go on I promise. I feel really upset over Robert because one can't live by writing & he must get some sort of job. He has got a wife and child to support.

And, in 1980, writing again to Deborah:

> [Robert] says he's to be 'the Lord Clark of the Slump, a series of telly programmes about 1930-31 of which he is compere […] I am DEVOTED to him.

In an interview with the Editor of the *Financial Times* in 2009, Skidelsky explained how his interest in Mosley originated in his fascination with politicians and the Slump. But he also admitted that it was driven by his friendship with his Oxford contemporary, Max Mosley, son of Oswald and Diana, and later with the whole family. 'Lowering his voice', he spoke 'of his own "calf-like" love for Max's mother and his fascination with Oswald, "a brilliant, charismatic man".'

Just how significant is someone's first piece of research in relation to the rest of their writing? Skidelsky stated that his biography of Mosley was 'emotionally centred' on the years covered by his dissertation – 1929 to 1931. Most of the controversy it aroused, he later admitted, was to do with his 'unduly benign treatment' of Mosley's later fascist phase. In 1993, no longer a member of the Labour Party but a Social Democrat, he commented that *Politicians and the Slump* had confirmed his bias towards 'Middle Way' thinking in politics and a disproportionate admiration for politicians with 'cross-party minds'. With hindsight he had 'lavished' his historical sympathies on the 'outsiders' – men such as Joseph Chamberlain, Lloyd George, Mosley and Churchill – because he identified with them. He admired them because of their outsized personalities and because they straddled the ground between Right and Left. But his writings also suggest that he admired them for battling against the suffocating atmosphere of late nineteenth-century liberalism. Does this simply reflect Skidelsky's obsession with the economic radicalism of Keynes? I disagree. Skidelsky always had a tendency to reject the pieties of the liberal establishment, even as a student. It seems more likely that his sympathy with outsiders stemmed from his background. The choice of his dissertation topic bore no relation to the interests of his tutors 'for whom British history stopped at 1914'. The fallout over his biography of Mosley was, however, another factor that probably helped to confirm his hostility to the liberal establishment he believed to have denied him an Oxford job. In 1993 he wrote that while obsessed with Mosley's 'passion for ideas so rare in an Englishman', he was loath to admit that Mosley had a 'dark side'. This approach would not be a problem with his prize-winning biography of Keynes because Keynes had not needed to espouse unacceptable means to achieve his radical aims. Determined to 'show the buggers', Skidelsky studied economics in order to write the biography. There he was able to put both his 'passion for ideas' and the genius of the economist centre stage.

Wendy Knowles has been an editor in Africa and the Caribbean and a publisher of children's books. She is currently researching biographies of people living in Ghana and Nigeria in the 1950s.

Juliet Miller

The Biographer's Need for a Body

Richard Long is a British artist with an international reputation who has been making and displaying his works for over forty years. Whilst still at art school, in 1967 he made 'A Line Made by Walking'. He took a train into the countryside, found a field full of daisies and walked in a straight line through the field. The resulting photograph of the line made by his feet brought him recognition as a member of the new generation of so-called conceptual artists. In 1989 he was awarded the Turner Prize. Now in his mid-sixties he still makes works both in the landscape and to be shown in galleries all over the world. In 2009 he had a major exhibition at Tate Britain. His work is directly or indirectly based on the walks he makes in landscape, with stones, rocks, mud, water and the features of the land as his creative tools.

Richard Long had, to my surprise, responded to my letter and agreed to meet me. He suggested the Arts Club. Making my way along Piccadilly with plenty of time in hand, I noticed a tall thin man ahead of me. He was wearing a knitted hat made of rough mountain wool that looked like it had once belonged to a yak; bought no doubt on one of his many foreign trips. His cotton jacket was frayed and worn and he had a sagging canvas rucksack on his back. The height was right, the clothes were right. Here was my biographical subject, the focus of my reading and thinking over the mildly obsessive previous six months. He was taking long strides and his thin frame bent forward as he walked. He had a distracted air as if his mind was far away from fume-ridden Piccadilly. I dodged around some tourists so as to keep this crucial body in view. Suddenly he took a turn to the right into the deserted Royal Academy courtyard and made his way to the front lobby. No longer protected by the crowds I felt exposed and hoped he wouldn't turn round and see me following him. This idea was of course fantastical as he had no idea what I looked like. But the one-sidedness of this intense pursuit suddenly made me feel a bit like a stalker. There were still twenty minutes before we were meant to meet, but here we both were in the wrong place. Apart from the two of us and a couple of people at the ticket desk, the front hall of the Royal Academy was deserted; what an awkward situation. Instead of introducing myself, I lost my nerve, felt ridiculous trying not to stare at him and took refuge in the ladies'.

When I came out there was no sign of my subject. Half an hour later, anxiously perched on a leather sofa in the agreed meeting place of the Arts Club, with no sign of the man in the yak hat, I wondered whether he had seen me following him into the R.A., disliked what he saw and made his way back home to Bristol. When I had convinced myself of this crazy idea and was about to leave, a tall thin upright man, casually but neatly dressed, sporting neither a hat nor a rucksack came up the stairs towards me and introduced himself. He said he was Richard Long and apologised for keeping me waiting. I believed him of course, but my image of the other Richard Long took a while to fade. I felt dislocated by the earlier mistake and by this entirely new person now sitting next to me on the sofa. How could I have allowed my imagination such free rein? I was intending to write about a living person not some fictionalised version. Here was the real man sitting next to me and listening attentively to what I had to say. Eventually, as we continued to talk, I had to admit to myself that through my absorption in the work and the artist I had created an imaginal body in which to house my own feelings and ideas. I had built my own Richard Long and until I *recognised* the *man in the hat* I hadn't been aware of how powerful this creation of mine had become. It seemed that it was important for me to have a visual form, a portrait of the person I was going to write about. Maybe this is always true and if the subject we are writing about is dead we hope for photographs or portraits because we need to know what they look like. Or maybe in this case, my *man in the hat* reflected deeper resonances of the ways in which Long communicates by arousing bodily sensations in those who look at his work. After months of looking at his art and with no images of the man himself to go on, I had built a body that had transmigrated onto a pavement in Piccadilly.

Unaware of the feckless way I had treated his physical self, Richard Long listened patiently to my responses to his work and generously agreed to be interviewed in his home outside Bristol. By the time I left him in the Arts Club my thoughts and enthusiasms were flowing steadily into the new body that I had been presented with and the *man in the hat* was beginning to be an embarrassing memory.

The question of why I needed to create the body of my biographical subject remains central to my writing about this artist. I do not think this would have happened if my subject was a writer or person of letters. The act of making art is a physical act and it is transmitted in a different way to the viewer than writing is to the reader. Richard Long's body and how he uses it are central to this. Long is an ectomorph. He is tall, wiry and strong. He has large feet and broad hands with long fingers. The fingers on his right hand are elegant but gnarled. The thumb nail is bent and disfigured. It is a hand that betrays its life history and its owner's purpose, yet his fingers also display a sensitivity and delicacy of touch. His hands have grown into the hands he needs them to be. They are representative of how his brain works and of his creative and imaginative self.

The artist's feet are as much part of his tool kit as his hands. I have only seen them encased in battered walking boots, pairs of which are piled up in his studio. The boots do not appear in Long's photographs, yet they are central to his work. Seeing them gave me the same sense of illicit excitement that any biographer might have on coming across her subject's worn pen or brushes. The boots are crucial because it is through walking that Long has discovered and refined his artistic purpose. On long walks he sleeps in a small tent and carries little with him except maps. He has a deep trust that his body will lead him to an idea or to a piece of work. Long has never wavered from his intuition that it is through his body that he knows what to do. 'The very first works I made were with my feet. Just with my left foot on the floor of a gallery. I have always thought of them as flat sculptures, two dimensional sculptures.'[1]

---

1 The quotes from the artist are from an interview with the author, 1.5.2010.

The Biographer's Need for a Body

Surrounded by the sterile conditions of a white-walled modern gallery, whilst I was looking at one of Long's photographs of works made in Africa, *Circle in Africa. Mulanje Mountain Malawi* I was taken aback by my response. I had the strange experience of smelling, not just in one intake of breath but many subsequent ones, the mixture of earth and body odours that I had previously only encountered in the African bush. As a psychotherapist I recognised this *smelling of an idea or feeling* from the emotionally charged atmosphere of my consulting room where senses may jump their normal neural pathways to force an unconscious affect to become conscious in the room. Sounds may be *heard*, smells *smelt* and images *seen*. Crucially this is not simply a mind process but a body process. It is one of the few times when we can truly experience what we may say to ourselves often, that mind and body cannot be separated. This is the body thinking. I cannot explain why I would have experienced this body knowledge by looking at a photograph, rather than being in the presence of another person, apart from the fact that I was very identified with the artist and his work spoke to me on this visceral level.

It may also be because Long uses his body as his pen or brush that he is able to communicate with his audience body to body and these strange crossed networks can occur. Long's body becomes the pen through which he inscribes the earth. It is by means of his body that the artist shows us his impact on the world and the world on him and through which he absorbs and digests the natural environment. 'My work involves touching in all different ways. It's touching the earth by walking. It's touching by leaving physical footprints that you can see. It interests me that I can use my body in different ways'.

I wonder in what other ways my body will reverberate as I proceed to write about this most moving of British artists.

Juliet Miller had a first career as a documentary filmmaker and a second as a Jungian analyst. She has published a book about female creativity and is currently interested in writing about contemporary artists and the ways in which they communicate with and affect their audiences.

Maureen Phillips

Mobile Home

I arrived at the entrance to the trailer park and checked the address Dad had given me over the phone. This was it – 555 Clayton Road. The numbers were printed on a shiny black plaque, much like what you'd see on a headstone in a cemetery. The plaque was attached to one of two granite pillars, each holding a long black wrought iron gate that looked like they had been opened remotely, allowing the driver to proceed. But these gates were fixed open—purely for show, not function.

Inching down the paved lane, I passed mobile homes with tidy little driveways, each with two cars parked neatly side by side. All of the homes displayed a patch of green grass in front, some brandishing brightly coloured gnomes or other garden ornaments. Checking the address on the seat beside me, I saw that Dad was in #4. I looked to my right and sure enough, there was #4 with Dad's perfectly clean blue Ford Galaxy and Rose's spotless red Ford Escort parked in front. I pulled in just behind them and got out. Dad was waiting by the open door and yelled over his shoulder to Rose, announcing my arrival.

'So these are the new digs', I said, glancing around as Dad took my jacket and hung it in the closet with the bi-fold doors in the small foyer.

'Yeah, we're pretty much moved in now. Just a few minor touches left to do. Rose! Where the hell are ya?'

Rose came mincing down the hall, looking flushed and freshly powdered, fluffing her short gray hair. She pecked me lightly on the cheek. I could smell her lipstick, knew she'd left a red kiss on my face, and discreetly thumbed it off.

'How are you, dear?' she said. 'Lovely to see you and so nice of you to come all this way'.

'I know … it's been a while, hasn't it. How long have you two been here now?'

'Six months on Saturday, dear. But never mind. Your father has all the small things taken care of now. It's pretty much all done. Come and sit down and have a cup of tea. I just made a fresh pot. And I've got some nice ginger cookies I bought at Safeway today'.

She disappeared into the kitchen just off the hallway and Dad gestured for me to sit down on the sofa. He was a shy man, and I could see he was struggling to think of something to say while Rose busied herself with the tea. With some effort, he lowered his ample girth into an overstuffed chair.

'So how are things at the university', he said. 'Busy, are ya?'

'Always busy, Dad'. I knew that was the answer he was looking for. No slackers in his family. Toil and make money – that was the goal. He'd worked all his life at the mill and was proud of what he'd accomplished. After Mum died, he sold our old house in the 'burbs and was living in an apartment when he met Rose at a Kiwanis bingo game. Rose, a single woman all her life, lived in an apartment complex too, so Dad moved into hers. They had been married for six years now and seemed to bring out the best in each other. But Rose wanted something more than an apartment. Not a whole house with a big garden, just something small and manageable where she could grow a patch of flowers. They had no luck finding anything close to what she wanted, so Rose came up with the idea of buying a mobile home after seeing an advertisement in the newspaper.

She came back from the kitchen with a tray full of tea paraphernalia and started pouring from the china teapot and offering us cookies from the box.

'So you were the one who found the trailer, Rose?' I asked, taking a cookie.

'Mobile home, dear', she corrected. 'Yes, I did. I'd had no luck at all finding a house small enough, and a mobile home seemed like the answer. We started looking right away, and when I saw in the newspaper that they were developing this mobile home park on the river, I said to your father we should go and have a look. There was a display unit all set up and we were both taken with it right away, weren't we, Ted?'

'Yep. Rose loved the place and they really had done a hell of a job on the display home. She took one look and said if they could give her exactly that, we'd take it'.

Rose looked at me and said, 'Finish your tea, dear, and I'll take you on a tour'.

I wiped the crumbs off my mouth with the paper napkin Rose had added to the tea tray and stood up. 'I'm all yours'.

Given we were in the living room, Rose started by pointing out the sofa and chair, nubbly-tufted in a pinky beige that perfectly matched the carpet and the curtains. There were two small faux wood tables holding a white-shaded lamp on each, and in front of the sofa stood a matching table that held the tea tray. No ornaments or framed photos graced any of the shiny surfaces. Against the wall loomed an armoire made of the same stuff as the tables, home to the TV and stereo. Next to the sofa I noticed a large woven basket piled high with balls of coloured wool; an orange ball placed on top had a pair of knitting needles stuck through with a small knitted sampler.

'Have you taken up knitting, Rose?'

'Oh heavens no, dear. I told the salesman in the display home that I wanted things exactly the same – *everything the same*. That basket of wool was part of the display, just as you see it now. Pretty, isn't it?' I agreed it was lovely.

We proceeded into the kitchen off the hall. The counter was spotless and uncluttered – not even a toaster or ersatz potted ivy in sight. On the table near the window sat a pair of tiny salt and pepper shakers in the shape of two white poodles. There was a shiny chrome kettle on the stove and hanging behind on the wall was a papier mâché rope of garlic. 'That's a nice touch, Rose. Did you make that?'

She answered somewhat impatiently, 'Honestly dear, no. That was in the display home too'.

As I followed my tour guide down the cream-carpeted hall, she introduced the bathroom on the left. Peeking in, I saw pale apricot-coloured walls, two towels in chocolate brown hanging on a chrome towel rack, and a fluffy chocolate mat lying in front of a gleaming white bathtub. On the wall next to the mirror over the sink hung two framed pictures of Little Bo Peep with her sheep. And in front of the mirror, reflecting back on itself, stood a large glass vase filled with imitation hydrangeas and stems of dried poppy seed heads.

I pointed at it and said, 'Like the display home?'

'That's right, dear. Just so'. I was starting to get the hang of it.

Leaving the bathroom, we finally reached the master bedroom at the end of the hall. A king-sized bed covered with a brown and white print bedspread in a swirly design resembling a cinnamon bun dominated the room. Oversized pillows with the same material were plumped up against a beige, plush buttoned headboard. On either side of the bed stood a small night table holding a brown lamp with a cream-coloured shade. My eyes passed over everything else and came to rest on a red book, lying open and face down under the lamp. Printed across the cover in gold letters read: *Pride and Prejudice.*

'Rose, that's an amazing coincidence! I'm in the middle of reading *Pride and Prejudice!*'

'Oh no, dear', she said. 'I'm not reading it. That's just the way they had it in the display home. Lying there, turned over … exactly like that'.

Maureen Phillips holds a Bachelor of Arts degree in English Literature from the University of British Columbia. She put her life on hold in Vancouver for the excitement and stimulation of pursuing an MA in Life Writing at UEA. She hopes one day to write her memoir.

Elizabeth Michelle Ruddick

The Conversation

Did Colette's and Violette Leduc's paths ever cross? In 1945, in spite of the differences between their ages, social status and careers, an encounter was not out of the question. Leduc certainly would have been aware of Colette's literary and civic accomplishments: fifty books published; the first woman admitted to the Académie Goncourt; a Chevalier of the Légion d'Honneur in recognition of her hospital work during WWI. Colette would have heard about the success of Leduc's first book, *In The Prison of Her Skin*, from mutual acquaintances such as Simone de Beauvoir, Jean Paul Sartre or Albert Camus. Part of the Paris *demimonde*, Leduc and Colette probably would have frequented the same bohemian haunts in which the following conversation might have been shared:

Violette Leduc is waiting for her mentor Simone de Beauvoir to meet her in the Café de Flore. When she arrives, Leduc complains about how difficult she finds it to write, how afraid she is her work will not be well-received.[1] Patient for as long as she can be, Simone de Beauvoir soon takes her leave. Frustrated by the brevity of their meeting, as well as the unrequited love she feels for de Beauvoir, Leduc lights another cigarette from the butt of her last and signals for more wine. At this moment, Colette enters the café, sees Leduc's gesture and mistakes it for an invitation to join her. The waiter and Colette approach Leduc simultaneously. Leduc asks for a second wine glass ...

---

1 Leduc, Violette. *La Batarde*, p. 241

'Mme. Leduc. We have often been in the same places, but ... well, now, here we are!'

Colette takes out her compact and opens it; satisfied with her reflection, she returns it to her purse and smiles as she seats herself.

'What a great pleasure, Mme. Colette,' Leduc greets her.

'Please forgive my appearance. I have been in such a rush today ...'

'To the contrary. You look very nice, indeed.'

'Well, I'm an old woman now, but I do my best.'

'I've never bothered much with my appearance. My mother convinced me that it wouldn't be of much use.'

'How ridiculous! My mother was just the opposite, telling me I was beautiful even when I was not.[2] She's been gone a long time now, but I miss her as if it were just yesterday.' *Colette pauses, looks around the room.* 'Are you luckier? Is your mother still alive? Do you see each other often?'

'Yes, she's alive, but I wouldn't say that was "lucky". She comes to Paris to shop and to see the men in her life.[3] She sees me only if it's convenient.'[4]

'Oh, what a pity. I don't know what I would have done without my mother's devotion. From her I learned about nature, love and life – she taught me, well, simply everything!'

'Surely, not everything!'

'Well, no ... not everything.' *Colette smiles at Leduc.* 'I wonder, have you read any of my books?'

'Of course. You are famous, Mme Colette. And so wise.

'You flatter me. I've learned through the years, of course, but my mother is the one who gave me the best advice: "There's only one person in this life you can count on, and that's yourself".'[5]

'I wish I could ... I'm never secure without someone in my life but ... my mother, perhaps, poisoned the well with her advice to "fly from all men".'[6]

---

2 **Colette**, *The Break of Day*, p. 23

3 **Leduc, Violette**, *In the Prison of Her Skin*, p. 62

4 **Leduc, Violette**, *Mad In Pursuit*, p. 211

5 **Thurman, Judith**, *Secrets of the Flesh: A Life of Colette*, p. xix, citing *Lettres a sa fille*.

6 **Leduc, Violette**, *La Batarde*, p. 222

'Yet you say she has men in her life ...'

'Yes. She needs someone around to admire her, and for her, appearance is everything. When I was a child, she brushed my hair three hundred strokes a day, three hundred and sixty-five days of the year.'[7]

'Mine, too! When I cut it off – and I was a woman of thirty! – she was furious. I had ruined her "masterpiece".'[8]

'At least you were her "masterpiece".' *Leduc drains her glass and refills it.* 'My mother never loved me.'[9]

'Surely that is not so ... but, in any event, I hope you found love elsewhere.'

'I have tried. With men and women.'

'Women, too ... ? How did you mother feel about that?'

'She didn't pay much attention to me. She knew nothing about my first lover at the Collège de Douai but my second relationship with the music teacher got her dismissed and me expelled. There was no way my mother could avoid knowing.' *Leduc pauses to refill Colette's wine glass and her own.* 'I left home not long after. What about yours? Was she upset by your involvements with women?'

'No. When I finally left my first husband Willy she thought anyone, male or female, would be an improvement. When I was with Missy, my mother told me she was glad that I had found someone who cared for me so tenderly.'[10]

'Tenderly ... For me, love is turmoil and disappointment. I find I am more comfortable with friends.'[11]

'I understand. Love is an illusion. That is why, after my first disappointments, I decided to expend myself on producing literature.'[12]

'Yes, exactly! I think that one must make love, die of love – the good

---

7 Leduc, Violette. *La Batarde*, p. 12

8 Thurman, Judith, *Secrets of the Flesh: A Life of Colette*, p. 24, quoting Colette.

9 Leduc, Violette, *In the Prison of Her Skin*, pp. 17, 53, 62, 86.

10 Thurman, Judith, *Secrets of the Flesh: A Life of Colette*, p.184

11 Leduc attached herself, primarily, to male homosexuals, among them, Jean Genet, Jean Cocteau and Maurice Sachs.

12 Colette, *The Vagabond*, p. 23.

The Conversation

part is that it is getting into training for writing. If you don't go through the mill, you may not have much material.'[13]

Colette and Leduc laugh together. They have both been through 'the mill'.

* * * * *

Colette, née Sidonie-Gabrielle Colette, was born on the 28th of January, 1873, in Saint-Sauveur-en-Puisaye, Yonne, to Adèle-Eugénie Sidonie Landoy ('Sido') and Jules-Joseph Colette. Violette Leduc was born on the 7th of April, 1907, in Arras, Pas de Calais, the illegitimate daughter of Berthe Leduc and the son of her mother's employer.[14] Neither the Colettes nor the Leducs were entirely acceptable to their provincial neighbors. Leduc's mother had no husband; Colette's was with her second. Both girls were raised in rural settings and as young women made lives for themselves in Paris. For Colette, when she married Henri Gauthier-Villars ('Willy') at twenty, the move was a jarring, painful separation from the countryside and the mother she adored. She had thoroughly enjoyed her childhood with three siblings to play with and a family that spoiled her.[15] Leduc, unfortunately, was an only and unwanted child who had received but slim nurturing from her grandmother Fideline.[16] For her, moving to Paris provided an escape both from the isolation of village life and her mother's contempt, but she did so alone.

For the ten years (1896-1906) Colette was married to Willy, fifteen years her senior, her social life was defined and circumscribed by his. When she wasn't writing the Claudine series of books, which Willy appropriated as his own, Colette was out with Willy, seeing and being seen, or, at his insistence and for his titillation, in bed with one of his mistresses. At thirty, fed up with Willy's infidelities, Colette moved in with Natalie Barney with whom she shared a brief sexual relationship

---

13 Leduc, Violette, *Mad In Pursuit*, p. 215

14 http://en/wikipedia.org/wiki/Violette Leduc

15 Thurman, Judith, *Secrets of the Flesh: A Life of Colette*, p. 20

16 http://en/wikipedia.org/wiki/Violette Leduc

and afterwards remained friends for life.[17]

For her literary success, Colette would have been welcome at Gertrude Stein's formal, arguably stuffy, salons. She certainly was included in Natalie Barney's uninhibited gatherings of radical women, many of whom, like Natalie, were unapologetic lesbians. It is here, perhaps, that Colette met Mathilde de Mornay, the Marquise de Belboeuf ('Missy'), and began their five-year relationship. During Colette's music hall adventures, described in *My Apprenticeships and Music Hall Sidelights*, it was their kiss in the performance of 'Egyptian Dream' which so scandalized the audience, future performances were cancelled.[18] Not long after, Colette and Willy divorced. Colette's enchantment with feminists and lesbians/separatists also cooled, although it was rumored she was involved for some time with the sensational Josephine Baker.[19]

In 1912, Colette married Henri de Jouvenel, editor of the newspaper *Le Matin*, with whom she had her only child, Colette de Jouvenel. There would be more scandal, after her five-year affair with her stepson Bertrand de Jouvenel was discovered, and, in 1924, another divorce. In 1935, when she was sixty-two, Colette married another younger man, Maurice Goudeket, and settled down. However, throughout her busy, if not chaotic, personal life, Colette always took care of herself. She drank socially, and moderately, and smoked only an occasional cigarette. During the music hall years, she had developed the habit of exercising and prided herself on being fit.[20] As for her work, no matter what was happening in her life, Colette wrote and wrote and wrote.

In contrast, Violette Leduc began her life in Paris in 1926 as a student at the Lycée Racine. After failing to pass her baccalaureate at the end of that first year, she found work as a telephone operator/secretary at Plon Publishing where she met Maurice Sachs and Simone de Beauvoir. Sachs is credited with persuading Leduc to pick up a pen and Simone de Beauvoir, with Jean Paul Sartre's help, for convincing Albert Camus at

---

17 http://en/wikipedia.org/wiki/Colette

18 Robinson, Christopher, *Scandal in the Ink*, p. 23

19 http://en.wikipedia.org/wiki/Colette, citing author Jean-Claude Baker's *Josephine: The Hungry Heart*

20 http://en.wikipedia.org/wiki/Colette

Éditions Gallimard to publish *In the Prison of Her Skin*, Leduc's first autobiographical book.[21] The publication captured the approval of Jean Cocteau and Jean Genet, among others, and was life-changing for Leduc whose first twenty years in Paris were bleak ones: 'The fly on my neck as I wash out my smock refuses to move. It's unpleasant, but I mustn't flick it off; it's a friend, it needs me. How alone must you be to want to keep, to protect a friend inside a fly.'[22]

Unlike Colette, Leduc was not a prolific writer: 'I write three notebook pages a day. It's too much and not enough … I am coveting the sweeper's broom, the street cleaner's wheeled bin along the rue Paul-Bert. I admire them: they have a job.'[23] Leduc, again unlike Colette, was anti-social, depressive and drank and smoked to excess.[24]

While Leduc continually spoke of her past, she resisted Simone de Beauvoir's suggestion that she use her memories in her writing. 'Yesterday she explained to me that I ought to try to remember Hermine and Gabriel, to tell that story the way I tell it to her …. But … that means remembering Isabelle, too ….'[25] Isabelle was Leduc's classmate and first lover; their affair ended when Isabelle graduated, and Leduc never got over it.

In 1939, after years alone in Paris, Leduc married Gabriel Mercier who was soon drafted. During the war, Leduc lived in the French countryside with Maurice Sachs who finally persuaded her to write: 'Your unhappy childhood is beginning to bore me to distraction … sit under an apple tree (and) write down all the things you tell me.'[26] When Leduc wasn't writing under the apple tree, she rode trains to Paris to sell black market goods. At the war's end, she returned to her flat, divorced Gabriel, and published her first autobiography. She would write and publish seven more.

---

21 Leduc, Violette, *La Batarde*, p.416

22 Leduc, Violette, *Mad in Pursuit*, p.85

23 Leduc, Violette, *Mad In Pursuit*, p.200.

24 Ibid., p.219

25 Ibid., p.241

26 Leduc, Violette, *La Batarde*, p.417.

Colette was the first woman to receive a national funeral for her contribution to French literature.[27] Leduc is still thought to be 'the most famous unknown author in France.'[28]

Elizabeth Michelle Ruddick is an unapologetic American who, before joining the UEA Life Writing programme, lived and practised law in Gloucester, Massachusetts. She holds a *Juris Doctor* from New England School of Law in Boston, Massachusetts and a Masters in Theological Studies from Harvard in Cambridge, Massachusetts. Currently at work on a biography of her mother, she hopes next to write her own memoir.

---

27 http:/en/Wikipedia.org/wiki/Colette
28 http://en/Wikipedia.org/wiki/Violette Leduc

Scriptwriting

Introduction by **Val Taylor**

Ed Amsden

Scott Brown

Joel Drake

Tamsin Flower

Shey Hargreaves

Tom O'Sullivan

Marianka Swain

Joe Wright

Do dramatic or comedic characters have to be likeable? In our marking criteria for the MA in Creative Writing: Scriptwriting, we ask that characters should be 'vivid, believable and engaging'. Some of our liveliest discussions around the workshop table turn upon what we mean by 'believable' and 'engaging'.

'Believable' depends upon the story world the characters inhabit; whether the writer has established the rules of the story world sufficiently to accommodate the characters, either as 'insiders' or 'outsiders' to it. 'Engaging' is more contentious. In everyday social discourse, to describe someone as engaging is usually complimentary; it suggests that there is something likeable about the person. In drama and comedy, however, we need to mine deeper seams.

Anti-heroes, for instance, often have dislikeable qualities or behaviours, but we do still invest in them, intellectually or emotionally. Villains are sometimes more pleasurable to watch than 'good guys'; we miss them when they exit and hanker for their return. Some characters, intended by their writers to attract the audience's empathy, instead try our patience. (I have a personal category labelled 'slappable' for them. It's heavily populated.)

Some characters, however, chill the blood, and it is this icy effect that holds us: the horrible sense of recognition, of their ugliness, but also of their truthful depiction. When such characters appear, I am reminded of Prospero's final acceptance of responsibility for Caliban, in *The Tempest*: '... this thing of darkness I/ Acknowledge mine.' They can be electrifying, but also profoundly disturbing. Confronted by them, we cannot exclaim, as Miranda does, about 'goodly creatures' or 'beauteous mankind', but we still must, ultimately, own them. Writers should introduce us to them all: the goodly, the beautiful, and the things of darkness. They are all ours.

VT

Ed Amsden

State of Things

INT. LIVING ROOM, DAY

A couple sit in silence in their small, dark living room.

MIKE, 58, is reading a television listings magazine which rests on his paunch. He wears glasses which he has to move down whenever he reads.

LESLEY, 53, is staring blankly towards the television. She has white hair and an absent expression.

The television is not on.

The clock ticks loudly.

> **LESLEY**
> Anything?

> **MIKE**
> No.

Lesley scratches her arm.

> **MIKE (CONT)**
> There's a list in here. Programmes
> coming up in the New Year.

> **LESLEY**
> Yeah?

Mike starts reading aloud.

> **MIKE**
> *Amanda Holden on for a Hero.*

> **LESLEY**
> What's that?

Mike reads closely.

> **MIKE**
> Concept undecided.

> **LESLEY**
> Right.

> **MIKE**
> *Katie Price is Right* – Jordan becomes
> Britain's answer to
> Judge Judy.

> **LESLEY**
> Hmm.

> **MIKE**
> *Judge Judy Finnigan.*

> **LESLEY**
> Sounds all right.

Mike glares at Lesley, disgust in his eyes.

He goes back to reading.

> **MIKE**
> *Tesco Extra*. On ITV2, Holly
> Willoughby reveals all the behind-
> the-scenes gossip from the staff-
> room of the Gillingham branch
> of Tesco.

Lesley lights a cigarette.

> **MIKE (CONT)**
> *Tesco Extras*. The staff of the
> Gillingham branch of Tesco act out
> sketches and skits from the Ricky
> Gervais sitcom *Extras*.

She takes a deep puff.

> **MIKE (CONT)**
> *Malcolm X Factor*.

Lesley splutters slightly on the cigarette.

> **MIKE (CONT)**
> *American History X Factor*.

She takes a sip from a glass of water.

> **MIKE (CONT)**
> *Bruce Willis is a Ghost*. Jonathan Ross
> ruins the endings of numerous
> films.

> **LESLEY**
> Are there any cookery shows?

Mike skim-reads the article.

> **MIKE**
> Erm … yeah. *Gok Wan's Wok Gang.*

> **LESLEY**
> Right.

They sit in silence.

The clock ticks louder.

> **MIKE**
> *Top Gear Casual Homophobia Special.*
> A repeat of any previous episode of
> the motoring show.

Lesley looks around her for the television remote.

> **MIKE (CONT)**
> *The World's Hardest Jigsaw* with
> Danny Dyer.

She is sitting on it.

> **MIKE (CONT)**
> *My 2 Cents with Neil Hamilton.*
> Hamilton gets all of his money
> converted to US dollars and counts
> how much there is.

She drags it from underneath herself.

MIKE (CONT)
Britain's Next Top Model Village.

She turns on the TV.

It shows a BBC One i-dent.

PRESENTER (V.O.)
And now on BBC One, *Who Do You
Think You Are?* In this week's
episode, Piers Morgan is asked to
explain himself.

FADE OUT.

Ed Amsden is an enthusiastic and imaginative writer of comedy, focusing on television sitcom in particular. Having completed a BA in English and Film at UEA, he progressed straight on to the Scriptwriting MA, where he has developed a wide range of disciplines. He is currently writing a sitcom about a pet crematorium, which he hopes to develop into a full series.

Scott Brown

Carnival Girls

Extract from episode one of a six-part series

FADE IN:

EXT. HIGH STREET, BUNTINGTON, KENT – DAWN

The tacky looking High Street of an old suburban market town in decline. Lampposts are draped in shabby Christmas – but not Christian specific – decorations and dead hanging baskets. A banner hangs across the street: 'BUNTINGTON OLDE WINTER FAYRE & PARADE – SAT 24TH DEC – 9AM+'.

The street is dark and deserted, except for KEN, 65. He's wearing woollies and a fluorescent jacket over many layers. He is pouring a coffee from a thermos flask into the plastic lid/cup and holds his clipboard between his legs.

Just as he's about to take his first sip, the headlights of an old transit van come into view behind him. He hears the van and – with the clipboard still between his legs – shuffles over to a litter bin. He balances the flask and cup on the domed top, retrieves his clipboard and jogs over to the middle of the street.

Using the clipboard, Ken makes a series of airport ground crew-style hand signals to guide the van into exactly the right place to park. When he is satisfied with the van's positioning, he gives a thumbs-up to the FIRST STALLHOLDER, 37, behind the wheel and heads back towards the bin. First Stallholder winds down his window.

>   **FIRST STALLHOLDER**
> Morning Ken!

>   **KEN**
> Yes, morning.

As Ken nears the bin, the cup and flask slide off the domed top. Ken runs and tries to catch it, but he's too slow and it spills everywhere. He stands over the pool of coffee, disappointed.

EXT. DRIVEWAY, CAROL'S HOUSE, BUNTINGTON – CONTINUOUS

A 1950s built semi-detached with an immaculately well-kept front garden. Chasing Christmas lights frame the glass panels around the wreathed front door.

INT. KELLY'S BEDROOM, CAROL'S HOUSE, BUNTINGTON – CONT.

In the darkness, the digital alarm clock reads '4:59'. After a moment, it turns to '5:00' and the alarm goes off. It sounds three times and the door swings open: light from the upstairs landing floods in around a silhouette. CAROL, 48, turns on the bedroom light as she surges in. She whips opens the curtains (still dark outside) and starts to tidy. KELLY, 16, remains hidden underneath the pink duvet of her single bed. Carol turns the alarm off, then bustles around the room.

>   **CAROL**
> Are you awake?

>   **KELLY**
> Hmm.

>   **CAROL**
> Are you awake?

> **KELLY**
> Hmmmmmm.

> **CAROL**
> Are you sure?

Carol waits for a moment and then turns on the alarm clock's radio: Mariah Carey, *All I Want For Christmas Is You*. A few seconds of Mariah as Carol stares at the body-shaped, duvet-covered mass. Carol turns up the volume. Kelly's head emerges.

> **KELLY**
> All right!

Carol turns the volume down. Kelly dives back under the duvet. Carol waits.

> **CAROL**
> I'll start hoovering.

After a moment, Kelly re-emerges and starts to get up.

> **CAROL (CONT'D)**
> Be downstairs in fifteen minutes.

Kelly looks at the alarm clock, Carol turns to go.

> **KELLY**
> Did you change my alarm?

> **CAROL**
> (as she goes)
> Half six is not enough time.

Carol shuts the door.

> **KELLY**
> (under her breath)
> For fuck's sake.

EXT. HIGH STREET, BUNTINGTON, KENT – LATER

Several more cars and vans have arrived. STALLHOLDERS are setting up on the pavements.

Ken is parking – 747 style again – an estate car and trailer driven by the SECOND STALLHOLDER. Ken repeatedly makes him move a few inches forwards and backwards. The Second Stallholder becomes irritated and revs the engine, causing the car to jolt forward a few feet. Ken leaps out of the way, gives the Second Stallholder a panicked thumbs-up and totters off.

INT. UPSTAIRS LANDING, CAROL'S HOUSE, BUNTINGTON – CONT.

From behind the closed bathroom door: the sound of running water from the shower. Carol jogs up the stairs, looking at her watch. When she reaches the landing, she knocks on the bathroom door as she opens it and pokes her head in.

> **CAROL**
> Five minutes!

Carol closes the door.

> **KELLY**
> (shouting from the shower)
> MUM!

The doorbell rings. Carol goes downstairs, increasing in volume with each step.

> **CAROL**
> Mary and Jenny are here!
> I'll make a start on her!

Carol is nearly at the bottom of the stairs.

> **CAROL (CONT'D)**
> FIVE MINUTES!

> **KELLY**
> (from the bathroom)
> I KNOW!

EXT. HIGH STREET, BUNTINGTON, KENT – LATER

Some Stallholders are still setting up, but most are finished. A stall's stereo is playing Paul McCartney's *Wonderful Christmastime*. Ken is stood next to a tinsel-clad burger van: bacon roll in one hand, clipboard in the other.

INT. KITCHEN, CAROL'S HOUSE, BUNTINGTON – CONT.

Carol's nicely designed – but small – modern kitchen.

JENNY, 16, is sitting on the middle of three stools positioned along the breakfast bar. She is wearing a pink dressing gown over joggers and a T-shirt. The counters and bar are completely covered with hairdressing equipment and make-up. Everything has been ordered in size and placed in straight lines. All the tongs, hairdryers and straighteners are placed on chopping boards and plugged into an elaborate arrangement of multi-socket adapters.

MARY, 49, leans against the counter at the back of the kitchen, nursing a mug of tea.

Carol is concentrating on curling Jenny's hair with tongs. Jenny is trying to eat a croissant. She breaks off a tiny piece and is just about to eat it.

> **CAROL**
> Don't move, please.

Jenny freezes, holding the bit of croissant a few inches from her mouth.

Kelly – also wearing a dressing gown – strops into the kitchen and sits on a stool.

> **CAROL (CONT'D)**
> Good morning.

Kelly stares forward.

> **MARY**
> Did you sleep well, Kelly?

Kelly gives Mary a withering look. Jenny eats the bit of croissant.

> **CAROL**
> Make the girls some tea, Mary.

Mary switches on the kettle.

> **KELLY**
> None for me.

Mary switches off the kettle.

> **CAROL**
> You should have something hot.

Mary switches on the kettle.

> **KELLY**
> I don't want it.

Mary switches off the kettle.

> **CAROL**
> It'll keep you warm later.

Mary switches on the kettle.

> **KELLY**
> I won't be able to wee when I'm in
> the dress, will I?

Carol shoots a warning look at Kelly. Mary switches off the kettle.

> **CAROL**
> You'd like some tea, wouldn't
> you Jennifer?

> **JENNY**
> No, thank you.

> **CAROL**
> You'll both be cold later.

Kelly and Jenny share a look.

> **CAROL (CONT'D)**
> I'll have a cup of tea then. Mine's
> gone cold.

Carol gives the mug to Mary. Mary pours the full – and still steaming – mug of tea into the sink and switches the kettle on.

After a moment, Carol glances up from Jenny's hair and stares at the kettle. Carol stops curling, places the tongs on the counter, switches off the kettle, picks it up and fills it from the tap. Once it is full, she slams it down on the counter for emphasis, takes up the straighteners again and resumes curling Jenny's hair.

After a moment, Mary switches the kettle on.

The girls look bored and tired. Carol straightens with intense concentration.

Scott Brown graduated from UEA's Scriptwriting and Performance BA in 2010 with starred first-class honours. He has worked professionally as an actor and stand-up comedian.

Joel Drake

Supermen
A Pilot

EXT. EMPTY PARKING LOT – DAY

A DOT APPEARS IN THE SKY ACROSS FROM VEG-A-MART SUPERMARKET. THE DOT GETS LARGER ACCOMPANIED BY A HUM.

INT. VEG-A-MART – DAY

TERRY, 56, MANAGER, **TED**, 16, HIS SON, **VERITY**, 22, ASSISTANT MANAGER, **STEVE**, 30, STOCK MANAGER, **LUCY**, 18, AND P**AUL**, 24, CASHIERS, STARE OUT OF THE FRONT WINDOW. A SHADOW FALLS ACROSS THEM.

> ***TERRY***
> Great god of guacamole.

EXT. EMPTY PARKING LOT – DAY

THE SPECK HAS BECOME A BUILDING DESCENDING BY THE AID OF GIANT ROCKETS. THE FRONT READS: 'BIG BIG WAREHOUSE.'

INT.VEG-A-MART – DAY

TERRY RUNS AROUND WAVING HIS ARMS.

> **TERRY**
> Chain store! Battle stations
> everyone!

> **PAUL**
> Should we ... ?

> **LUCY**
> Battle stations are when Terry hides
> under his desk.

A BOOM AND FLASH. EVERYONE JUMPS.

EXT. PARKING LOT – DAY

BIG BIG WAREHOUSE DIGS INTO THE GROUND. THE BUILDING
TRANSFORMS. LAMPPOSTS SPROUT UP. THE BUILDING FOLDS OUT. THE
TRANSFORMATION COMPLETES. CUSTOMERS PARK AND FLOCK INSIDE.

INT. VEG-A-MART – DAY

> **LUCY**
> It must die.

SHE EXITS. STEVE AND PAUL FOLLOW. TERRY RUNS AWAY TO HIS OFFICE,
VERITY IN PURSUIT.

EXT. BIG BIG WAREHOUSE – DAY

LUCY, STEVE AND PAUL LOOK UP AT BIG BIG WAREHOUSE. IT GLOWS
AND HUMS EERILY.

> **STEVE**
> They have. THE. Best. Nachos.

> **LUCY**
> You can feel the evil.

> **PAUL**
> Yeah. But people know better than
> to shop at a place like this, right?

MRS NESSBAUM, 42, EXITS WITH A CARTLOAD OF DIAPERS. EYES WILD.

> **MRS NESSBAUM**
> HEY VEG-A-MORONS! GOTS ME
> FOUR HUNDRED DIAPERS FOR
> TWENTY DOLLARS!

> **STEVE**
> But, Mrs Nessbaum, you don't even
> have, like … a baby.

> **MRS NESSBAUM**
> I'M GONNA MAKE SOME!

INT. NESSBAUM MINIVAN – DAY

MR NESSBAUM, 46, SHAKES WITH FEAR.

EXT. BIG BIG WAREHOUSE – DAY

> **PAUL**
> What's her problem?

> **STEVE**
> Sale Madness, man!

> **PAUL**
> Excuse me?

> **LUCY**
> Superlow prices have put normal shoppers into a state of hyper-consumerism. We call it ... 'Sale Madness.'

> **PAUL**
> Well, then I guess we should check it out.

> **LUCY**
> And destroy it.

> **STEVE**
> And nachos!

INT. TERRY'S OFFICE – DAY

TERRY HIDES UNDER HIS DESK. VERITY MID-PEP TALK.

> **VERITY**
> C'mon Ter-Bear! Positive fulfillment! Actuate your chi! Oooommmmmm.

> **TERRY**
> I hate chi.

> **VERITY**
> No you don't! You hate bats, toenails –

> **TERRY**
> And chi! It's over, Verity! We might as well quit! Who's gonna come here when they can go to Big Big Warehouse?

> **VERITY**
> What about the locavores!?

INT. VEG-A-MART – DAY

A **HIPSTER**, 33, POINTS TO 'LOCAL FOOD AISLES' SIGN AND BERATES TED.

> **HIPSTER**
> More like the BRITISH AISLES!

INT. TERRY'S OFFICE – DAY

> **VERITY**
> OK. We'll have to get competitive!
> Dust the fruit, paint new signs, set
> traps for the honey badger! What
> about our website?

> **TERRY**
> We have a website?

> **VERITY**
> Doesn't everything?

THEY PULL UP THE VEG-A-MART SITE: DINKY, WITH A FEW RANDOM GIFS. NO USEFUL INFORMATION. AN ANNOYING JINGLE LOOPS.

> **TERRY**
> Aww! Little cows! Look!

> **VERITY**
> … Let's see what we're up against.

BBW WEBSITE: IT'S SLICK WITH TONS OF ANIMATION.

P.H.A.R.O.S. (PLEASANT AND HELPFUL ALL-SEEING OVERLORD SYSTEM), BBW'S SPOKESMAN, GREETS THEM.

> ### *P.H.A.R.O.S.*
> Welcome! You have WON: a potato!

> ### *TERRY*
> I won!

> ### *VERITY*
> Terry! It's the enemy!

> ### *TERRY*
> But I never win.

> ### *VERITY*
> Wait … That's it! We'll have a
> contest! And the winner gets a
> free prize!

> ### *TERRY*
> How free? Like, free-free?

> ### *VERITY*
> Hush! Now what contest to have?
> Beauty pageant? … Been done. Cat
> show? … Drama. Talent show? …
> Mimes. I know! Doggies! PERF!
> We'll have a Doggie-Beauty-Pageant-
> Show!

> ### *TERRY*
> That's … confusing.

> ### *VERITY*
> And you, me and Betsy will judge!

TERRY WHIMPERS.

VERITY (CONT'D)
Don't be a baby! Let's get to it!

INT. BIG BIG WAREHOUSE

PAUL AND LUCY STAND BEFORE A CITY OF PRODUCTS.

P.H.A.R.O.S. ON SCREENS EVERYWHERE. SHOPPERS FIGHT OVER DEALS. PAUL PICKS UP AN ITEM.

PAUL
Ten pounds of pancake mix for a
dollar? How is this possible?

LUCY
Puppy labor.

PAUL
Say what now?

LUCY
It says on the package 'Made with
Puppy Labor'. It even has a picture.

SHE HOLDS UP A BAG OF PANCAKE MIX WITH A PICTURE OF A PUPPY WEARING AN EYEPATCH.

PAUL
But ... Thumbs. And ... Who would
want to buy such evil products?

MRS NESSBAUM NOW HOLDS THE BAG OF PANCAKE MIX.

MRS NESSBAUM
BABIES LOVE PANCAKE MIX!

INT. NESSBAUM MINIVAN – DAY

MR NESSBAUM SOBS IN A MINIVAN FILLED WITH DIAPERS.

INT. BIG BIG WAREHOUSE – DAY

STEVE ARRIVES STUFFING HIS FACE WITH NACHOS.

> **STEVE**
> (mouth full)
> I got nachos!

> **PAUL**
> Steve, don't! Evil!

> **STEVE**
> (crestfallen)
> But. Nachos!

LUCY EXAMINES THE NACHOS.

> **LUCY**
> These aren't even made with cheese.

STEVE CONTINUES TO STUFF HIS FACE.

> **STEVE**
> Terrible! Just terrible!

> **LUCY**
> Or corn.

STEVE SHAKES HIS HEAD. CONTINUES EATING.

> **LUCY (CONT'D)**
> But it does have 'meat bits.'

STEVE STOPS MID-MUNCH.

> **STEVE**
> Meat?

> **LUCY**
> Bits.

STEVE TREMBLES. HIS EYES GO CRAZY. THE NACHOS DROP.

> **PAUL**
> You there Steve? Steve.

> **LUCY**
> Steve's a very strict vegetarian.

STEVE FOAMS AT THE MOUTH.

> **LUCY (CONT'D)**
> Very. Very. Strict.

STEVE LETS OUT A CRY. HE KNOCKS ITEMS OFF SHELVES, TEARS AROUND THE STORE SCREAMING AT CUSTOMERS.

> **PAUL**
> I see.

MIDWAY THROUGH WRECKING THE CEREAL AISLE, A METAL CLAW GRABS STEVE: ONE OF P.H.A.R.O.S.'S DRONES.

> **P.H.A.R.O.S.**
> What are you doing, Steve?

> **STEVE**
> (still mad)
> How did you know my name, guy?

P.H.A.R.O.S.
You are wearing a nametag.

STEVE
Maybe I am!

P.H.A.R.O.S.
Please cease your destructive
activities.

STEVE
No way robo-dude!

HE STRUGGLES WILDLY IN THE GRIP OF P.H.A.R.O.S.

P.H.A.R.O.S.
Oh dear. Perhaps music will
calm you.

P.H.A.R.O.S.'S SCREEN TURNS INTO A JUKEBOX. SOFT POP PLAYS IN THE
STORE. CUSTOMERS LOOK ENTICED BY SMOOTH BEATS. BOY BAND
'YEAH YEAH'S. FOG POURS FROM THE STOCKROOM DOORS. THE
'STOCKBOYS', A 4-PART BOY BAND STRUT OUT.

STOCKBOY 1
Oh baby, you've done it again (oooh)
Smashed my life on the floor (yeah)
But I can't let you in again (girl)
the way I did before (no no no)

**DANCE INTERLUDE. LADIES SWOON. MEN SWOON. STOCKBOYS
DANCE STEVE TOWARDS THE FRONT.**

STOCKBOY 2
So it's time for you to go (oh)
get you outta my head (please) and

if you try to come back for more
(girl) please remember these words
that I said:

ALL STOCKBOYS
This is a clean-up on aisle three,
'cause it's over with you and me
(me) if you come back here again,
I tell you my friend you will regret
you messed with me (ooh). You
will regret you messed with me
[Repeat x3].

EXT. BIG BIG WAREHOUSE – DAY (CONTINUOUS)

THE STOCKBOYS THROW STEVE OUT THE FRONT DOOR.

STOCKBOY 1
ME!

INT. BIG BIG WAREHOUSE – DAY

P.H.A.R.O.S. MENACES LUCY AND PAUL.

P.H.A.R.O.S.
Now, are we going to have any
more trouble? Or would you like
an encore?

PAUL
Please no.

P.H.A.R.O.S.
Excellent. Have a coupon for a
potato!

> **PAUL**
> I don't actually need –

P.H.A.R.O.S. PUTS THE COUPON INTO PAUL'S POCKET.

> **P.H.A.R.O.S.**
> I insist! Big Big Warehouse's deals
> are the best, I assure you. And if you
> find a better deal on a potato we
> match it.

LUCY GRABS P.H.A.R.O.S. BY THE SCREEN AND SHAKES HIM.

> **LUCY**
> Listen Speak-N-Spell, you're not
> wanted here! Capiche?

> **P.H.A.R.O.S.**
> Ss-stop s-sshaking m-me I'mmmm
> ffff –.

> **LUCY**
> Huh? You're a f-f-frisbee? Really?

SHE FRISBEES P.H.A.R.O.S. INTO THE RAFTERS. HE BOUNCES AROUND, GETS STUCK, TWITCHES. THEN BURSTS INTO FLAMES.

> **LUCY (CONT'D)**
> We can go now.

> **PAUL**
> Yes'm.

THEY WALK BY THE COWERING STOCKBOYS AND OUT THE DOOR.

EXT. BIG BIG WAREHOUSE – DAY

STEVE WAVES AT LUCY AND PAUL.

> **STEVE**
>Hey guys! Hey!

STEVE SEES SOMETHING.

> **STEVE (CONT'D)**
>Lucy! Look out!

LUCY TURNS. A POSSE OF SHOPPING CARTS ROLLS TOWARDS HER. HER EYES NARROW. SHE TAKES A FIGHTING STANCE.

> **PAUL**
>The hell?

> **LUCY**
>Get some, you overgrown colanders!

THE SHOPPING CARTS ADVANCE ON HER. SHE JUDO KICKS AND SENDS ONE FLYING. THE CARTS ENCIRCLE HER. SHE TURNS AND TURNS. ONE OF THE CARTS REARS UP AT HER. SHE BLOCKS. LUCY THROWS THE NEXT ATTACKER. THE CARTS RUSH INWARD.

> **PAUL**
>Look out!

LUCY LEAPS OVER THE CARTS. LETS OUT A WAR CRY AND LANDS ON HER FEET, READY TO FIGHT. THE CARTS PULL BACK.

> **LUCY**
>Giving up? Cowards!

THE CARTS PULL INTO A GROUP. THEY DISASSEMBLE AND TRANSFORM: LEGS, BODY, ARMS AND HEAD FORM A GIANT REPTILIAN MONSTER … CARTZILLA. IT ROARS IN ANGER LETTING OUT A BLAZE OF FIRE.

> **PAUL**
> Wanna run away?

> **LUCY**
> Maybe … Yeah.

THE TRIO RUN FOR IT. CARTZILLA PURSUES THEM. THEY BARELY MAKE IT TO THE EDGE OF THE PARKING LOT WHERE THE ANTI-THEFT LINE STOPS CARTZILLA. HE ROARS, FURIOUS. LUCY BLOWS A RASPBERRY AND EXITS. CARTZILLA PETULANTLY KICKS A MINIVAN AND SLUMPS OFF. MR NESSBAUM, WHO WAS SITTING IN THE MINIVAN, SCREAMS.

INT. VEG-A-MART – DAY

LUCY, STEVE AND PAUL ENTER AND FIND A RUNWAY IN THE STORE. LIGHTS. MUSIC. VERITY AND HER PAPILLON, BETSY, SIT AT THE JUDGES' TABLE DECKED OUT IN PINK FRILLS. A FAT BLACK LAB SITS ON TERRY. FIVE CUSTOMERS WATCH.

> **VERITY**
> Next up: Mrs Grossman and Fritz!

ENTER THE SEVERE **MRS GROSSMAN**, 45, AND **FRITZ**, 3, GERMAN SHEPHERD, IN TUTUS. FRITZ GROWLS AND FIGHTS. **MR GROSSMAN,** 50, APPLAUDS.

> **VERITY (CONT'D)**
> Very nice *Swan Lake* theme! Love the
> sequins! Talent?

> **MRS GROSSMAN**
> Fritz! Kill!

FRITZ GOES AFTER MR GROSSMAN.

> **VERITY**
> Thank you! Next up: Mr Lee and
> Barnaby! Yay!

SHE CLAPS BETSY'S PAWS TOGETHER.

> **STEVE**
> I hope you guys are seeing this.

VERITY SEES THE TRIO.

> **VERITY**
> Paulie! Stevie! Lucy-ie! We're having
> a Doggie-Beauty-Pageant-Show!

> **PAUL**
> I see … Why?

> **VERITY**
> To attract customers!

FRITZ GOES BY IN PURSUIT OF MR GROSSMAN.

> **PAUL**
> About that. We've just been over to
> Big Big Warehouse. And –

> **VERITY**
> They're trembling in their boots?

> **PAUL**
> I don't think your doggie … thingy
> is going to work.

VERITY TEARS UP.

> **VERITY**
> B-but, D-Doggie-Beauty-P-Pageant!

LUCY AND STEVE HIDE.

> **PAUL**
> It's not going to be enough. They're
> just too big. I'm sorry –

> **VERITY**
> No you're not! You're so smart but
> you don't really care! I care! And
> caring is what will save us.

VERITY COLLECTS HERSELF.

> **VERITY (CONT'D)**
> Now, I'm going to finish my
> pageant, and save Veg-A-Mart!

SHE STOMPS AWAY. LUCY AND STEVE ARE BACK.

> **LUCY**
> Way to make my sister cry dude.

> **PAUL**
> But ... It's the truth.

> **LUCY**
> Dude. She's having a Doggie-Beauty-
> Pageant. You think she cares about
> truth?

> **STEVE**
> Beauty is truth!

> **LUCY**
> Why don't you put that college
> brain of yours to use already?

> **PAUL**
> What can I do? I'm just a cashier.

> **LUCY**
> What happened man? You were a
> hero in this town. Now look at you:
> couldn't even turn down a coupon
> from the enemy. Let's go, Steve.

THEY EXIT. PAUL PULLS THE COUPON OUT.

> **PAUL**
> It was only for a potat – !

SOMETHING STRIKES HIM.

> **PAUL (CONT'D)**
> Oh.

INT. VEG-A-MART BACK ROOM – DAY

LUCY PLAYING A GAME AT THE COMPUTER, STEVE 'HELPING'.

> **STEVE**
> Right there! Mage! Get the mage!
> The mage! Get him! Lucy get him!
> Mage!

> **LUCY**
> Freaking calm down!

PAUL ENTERS.

> **PAUL**
> I got it guys! I know what to do!

THEY STARE BLANKLY.

> **LUCY**
> 'Bout what?

> **PAUL**
> Our store? The conversation we
> just had?

> **LUCY**
> Oh.

SHE GOES BACK TO THE GAME.

> **PAUL**
> What ... ? Never mind, I need
> the computer.

> **STEVE**
> But mages!

> **PAUL**
> Mages later Steve.

INT. BIG BIG WAREHOUSE – DAY

LUCY, PAUL AND STEVE GO UP TO P.H.A.R.O.S. CHECKOUT DRONE.

LUCY
Hey there Etch-A-Sketch.

P.H.A.R.O.S.
Well! How did you get past
Cartzilla?

EXT. BIG BIG WAREHOUSE – DAY

VERITY AWARDS A 'MISS CONGENIALITY' RIBBON TO CARTZILLA AND
CLAPS HER HANDS.

VERITY
Yaaaayy!

CARTZILLA ROARS IN JOY. MR GROSSMAN PASSES, CHASED BY FRITZ.

INT. BIG BIG WAREHOUSE – DAY

P.H.A.R.O.S.
And the Stockboys?

EXT. BIG BIG WAREHOUSE – DAY

THE STOCKBOYS SING *SEXUAL HEALING* OUTSIDE A ROCKING NESSBAUM
VAN.

P.H.A.R.O.S.
Clever. Well what do you want?

PAUL
Not much, I just found a better deal
for a potato.

HE PUTS DOWN A VEG-A-MART COUPON FOR INFINITY PERCENT OFF A
POTATO. P.H.A.R.O.S. SCANS IT. BEEP. SCANS AGAIN. ERROR ALARM.

> **P.H.A.R.O.S.**
> But that's-th-
> thaaaaaaaaaaauuuhhhhzzzz

P.H.A.R.O.S. SMOKES AND TWITCHES. SPARKS FLY.

> **PAUL**
> What's amatter? Does not compute?

THE WHOLE STORE STARTS TO MALFUNCTION.

> **PAUL (CONT'D)**
> I think ... Let's run.

EVERYONE RUNS OUT OF BIG BIG WAREHOUSE.

EXT. BIG BIG WAREHOUSE – DAY

SMOKE POURS FROM THE BUILDING AS IT DE-TRANSFORMS. LAMPPOSTS SUCK INTO THE GROUND. ROCKETS START LIFT OFF. BBW EXPELS THE LAST CUSTOMERS AND TAKES OFF INTO THE SKY.

> **PAUL**
> Woo! It worked! Hey guys!
> High five!

LUCY AND STEVE ARE WALKING BACK TO VEG-A-MART.

> **STEVE**
> Mages!

> **PAUL**
> Go me ... Yeah.

END OF PILOT

Joel Drake grew up in suburban Massachusetts. In 2007 he graduated from Occidental College in Los Angeles, California. For the next three years he worked in television for various production companies. In 2010 he moved to Norwich to attend UEA's prestigious Creative Writing programme.

Tamsin Flower

Compound Education
Scenes from a play in progress

ACT 1, SCENE 4

Bahrain (1996), St Christopher's British School playground. Nora (14), a slight and frightened Brit stands facing Jen (14), a flame-haired, big-boned Australian. The air is heavy with dust and moisture as it nears mid-day. Picnic tables, alcoves and distant Portakabins interrupt the expanse. Curiously, an archaeological dig clutters one corner. Jen has been ordered by the formidable Ms Cray to show Nora around her new school.

Jen

So you may as well tell me about
yourself. How old are you?

Nora

Fourteen.

Jen

You look younger. Is that an Alice
band you're wearing?

Nora

Yeah.

Jen

Thought so. Are you wearing sun-block on your face?

Nora

No.

Jen

Didn't think so. You'll look like Red Rock Canyon tonight.

Nora

Do you have some?

Jen

No, and if I did, I wouldn't borrow it out. Everyone'd want some.

Jen lazily points to the picnic tables.

This is where some people eat their lunch.

Some people, the chicken-shits eat in the cloisters over there – some Greek girls ... and the geeky Arab guys. The Asians eat in the library.

Nora

Why?

Jen

I dunno. The Asians eat in the library, that's how it is. It's like an old women's meeting in there.

Nora
Are there a lot of Asian people?

Jen
Why, d'you like 'em?

Nora
I was just interested.

Jen
You don't have to be. *(Smirks.)*
There's mainly Americans and
Australians and whingeing poms
out here in the playground.

Studies Nora.

You know what whingeing poms is?

Nora shakes her head.

You. British. Where in merry
England do you come from
anyways?

Nora
Nottingham.

Jen
Oh yeah, what's there?

Nora
A castle. And there's a … an old
market with lace weavers and –

Jen

Yeah OK.

Jen sees Melissa (a gang member) in the distance.

Hey Melissa! Babe! Wait there.
(To Nora.) Don't move a muscle.

Jen goes to talk to Melissa conspiratorially. Nora is drawn to the 'dig' and looks more closely. The Dilmun period God sculpture mentioned in assembly, sits on a plinth. She circles it. As she does so a boy of roughly the same age emerges from hiding among the artefacts. There is an ethereal quality about his mixed Arabic-European features. He has been crying and holds an old, woven fishing-trap in his hands.

Isa

Do you like him?

Nora

Oh! Sorry, I didn't know you were
there. Is it a him?

Isa

He's a Ram, so yes.

Nora

How do you know?

Isa

My father dug him up.

Nora

Does he work here?

Isa

Yep, this is all his.

Nora

Really?

Isa

No, not really. It's all government property. They don't care though. We could substitute everything with Lego and they wouldn't know the difference.

Nora

(Laughs.)

Isa

It's funny, but wouldn't you want to know what you own?

Nora

I don't own anything.

Isa

Yes you do.

Nora

I have some porcelain dolls, they're expensive.

Isa

Then own them. I'm Isa.

Nora

Nora.

Isa

Nice to meet you. You look new.

Nora
Brand new today.

Isa
Who's showing you around?

Nora
Jenny Masterson.

Isa
Where is she now?

Nora
Over there with a girl.

Jen notices Isa staring at her.

Jen
Don't stare at me worm, I know
you're fucking in love but deal with
it.

Isa
Don't call me that.

Jen
(Approaching)
What's that worm-boy?

Isa
My name's Isa, don't call me that.

Jen
OK worm. Look, if you two wanna
hang out together, don't let me get

in the way.
(Sees Isa's basket.)
Er! What's that piece of shit?

Isa

A 1000-year-old fish-trap.

Jen

Looks like a basket to catch heads
in. You better watch out. OK, I'll tell
Miss Cray you're with Isa all right?

Nora

Yep, OK.

Jen and Melissa amble offstage.

Isa

She thinks she owns the school. She
does.

Nora

Why?

Isa

Look at her, she could crack a skull
with her tongue.

Nora

She's not that scary.

Isa

Not yet.
(Grins)
Her mother's chairman to the
Governors. They own the place.

Nora

(Indicates the godhead.)
Why do they let it just sit like that?
Anyone could vandalise it.

Isa

Vandalise? Hmmm. One, they don't
care cause it's government property
and two, have you met Miss Cray?
No one wants to be in her office.
She could stick a stiletto through
your heart and roast it if she wants.

Nora

(Chuckles.)
She seemed fair enough.

Isa

She seems a lot of things.
(Gestures to God statue.)
If you stare at the God-face long
enough you can see it smile.

Nora

Oh!

Isa

Or grimace, whichever.

Nora

Looks like a mask.

Isa

Yeah it's all like that, they didn't
think in 3-D, the Dilmuns.

Nora

I'm not sure I think in 3-D. Isn't it a
10-D thing?

Isa

Ha! Don't let Jen know you're
bright.

Nora

But if you're just nice and chatty,
surely –

Isa

Just keep quiet, it's easier.

Nora is subdued. A Mullah sings prayers from a nearby mosque.

Nora

This is a weird adventure.

Isa

A big one though, here –

Isa gives Nora a piece of pottery from the dig's findings.

– have it, polish it. It's been buried
long enough.

Nora

That's amazing! Thank –

Enter Ms Cray. As she approaches, they fall silent.

Ms Cray

Isa, I know this is your father's dig,
but it doesn't mean you can riffle
through it during morning break.

Isa
I wasn't riffling.

Ms Cray
OK Isa, that's enough.

Isa
We were just talking.

Ms Cray
Erm, what did I say?
Have you been sobbing Isa?

Isa
Yes.

Ms Cray puts a hand on Isa's shoulder.

Now, I know your mother's leaving
the island soon. Is that right?

Isa nods.

Ms Cray
But sharing your upset with Nora on
her first day isn't appropriate, is it?

Isa does not respond.

What impression does that give?

Isa
(Mumbles.)
I don't know.

Ms Cray
Sorry, what was that?

Isa
I. Don't. Know.

Ms Cray
Well, not a *kind* one Isa.

Nora
I like being shown the artefacts.

Ms Cray
Hmmm, but we can't do what we
like all the time can we?

Ms Cray takes a tissue from her pocket and hands it to Isa.

Here. She hasn't left yet has she?

Isa
She's not going to.

Ms Cray
Al Jazeera TV's banned, she'll have
to. Now, the sooner you get used
to that, the easier it'll be. Norah
what's ..? Isa, go and wash your
face, there's a good man.

They watch him lope offstage.

Ms Cray
Give me that please.

Ms Cray indicates the ceramic piece Isa has given Nora. It has left a dirt-mark on her skirt. Nora hands it over and Ms Cray pockets it.

Your next class is Home Economics.
Cheer up! Do you like cooking?

Nora

I'm not very good at it.

Ms Cray

Good, you can learn. I'll show you
the way. You know, Isa's a very
friendly young man, very, what
you'd call 'sensitive'. But it's
important you have an overall view
of the school. Especially as your
father's teaching here. Now, see
that?

Ms Cray points to a utilitarian building.

Nora

Yes.

Ms Cray

That's going to be the new art
block. The governors put a lot of
money into ensuring you have the
very best of everything. Don't you
feel lucky?

Nora

Yes.

Ms Cray
So scrabbling about in the dirt isn't
what well-educated people do.
That's what they do in the villages,
they aren't so lucky. Now, you will
find everyone here very helpful and
friendly. There's just one thing you
need to give back, in this mutual
contract of ours Nora.

Pause.

Do you know what it is?

Nora
Hard work.

Ms Cray
Hard work, yes, but I was thinking
more of – abiding by the rules.
That way everyone's happy. Follow
the rules and we'll give you
everything you need. It's an exciting
place, isn't it?

Nora
Yes, thank you.

End of Scene

ACT ONE, SCENE 6

8pm in Al-Zamil compound. The temperature is dropping. Viki (a 15-year-old-Brit) leads the way to the compound garden, showing Jen and Mel (a 15-year-old Aussie) where they can make themselves comfortable. Nora follows. The group carry towels to sit on, four bottles of cider and two bottles of vodka. They settle near the pool changing rooms.

Jen

Where shall we keep this booze, eh?

Mel

Shhhhush!

Jen

What!? You think they fuckin' care?
The gardeners are probably
dribbling at us in our shorts.

Viki

Don't.

Jen

What?

Viki

It's my compound, I see them
every day.

Jen

Oh yeah? What's the name of
that one?

Viki

Where?

Jen

That one, hiding behind the
hedge there.

Viki

Shut up!

Jen

Sorry babe, couldn't resist.

Viki

Urgh! Don't. They're all old men.

Jen

Even the maids?

Viki

Yeah, ours has sideburns!

Mel, Viki and Jen laugh.

Jen

You got a maid?
Nora? Loner? You got a maid?

Nora

No, we don't want one.

Jen

Yeah, that happens. People come
here and get all high and mighty
but the fact is if you don't pay 'em
peanuts, they'll have to eat dirt
from some other nasty bastard's
hand. Int that right Mel?

Mel

(Nods)
This is boring.

Jen

Yeah, Nora, come over here. You got
the bottles ready Mel? OK, so it's
half however many we say, getting
faster.

Mel

OK.

Jen, Mel & Viki:

One two	(they drink)	you look like poo
Three four	(they drink)	drink like a whore
Five six	(they drink)	show those dicks
Seven eight	(they drink)	pull your weight
Nine ten	(they drink)	start again

Jen

Ready!

They gollop from their bottles, swilling cider in their mouths while counting to ten on their fingers. As they spray each other with saliva-diluted cider, Nora climbs up a date-palm onto the changing-room roof.

Jen

You don't seem to be drinking?
Don't fancy being spat on huh?

Nora

I'm fine, just watching.

Jen

Fuckin' weirdo. Come here –

Mel

Jen.

Jen

Come here, I wanna talk to you. Or you scared of me for real? Come –

Nora climbs down and sits near them.

Jen

These girls wanna get to know you, right?

Mel and Viki nod.

So, to be straight with you, you're never gonna feel part of the group unless you share stuff with us. Let's have a sharing!

Viki

Ooooh me first!

Jen

Go ahead Viksta!

Viki

OK, you don't know this but … I have a little crush on Mr Sutcliff.

Jen

We know!

Mel

Yeah, tell us something interesting.

Viki

And ... and I kept his pen when he lent it to me.

Jen

You freak, does it smell of him?

Viki

Yes.

Jen

Ha ha! Mel ... you enjoying yourself Nora?

Nora

Yeah.

Mel

You don't know this but loverboy's getting a pack of needles from the kids over at the American school.

Jen

You don't say. He's gonna make a killing on the sixth formers. You're looking a little shocked Nora?

Nora

No.

Jen

But see we trust you. Now I've got one, right.

I ... I listened in on a meeting at our
house about Mr Sudbury. There is
some serious shit going down and
he's going with it! *(Looks at Nora.)*
See no secrets here.
What *you* got?

Nora

I don't know, I don't have any
secrets.

Jen

You gotta have something otherwise
you might not be human. Maybe
you're not.

Nora

Well,

(They smile attentively.)

I used to fake migraines to get out
of PE.

Jen

Jesus, is that all you've got? Never
mind. Pass the girl some juice.

Mel reaches for a bottle of vodka and passes it to Nora, who resists.

Nora

I –

Jen

A little bit won't hurt, OK?

Mel

Yeah, live a little.

Viki

It's good.

Jen

Do it straight mind, I mean we did
ten straight.

Nora drinks from the bottle of vodka.

Mel

Wah!

Others

Hooooooo!

Nora

(Laughs, encouraged.)
There is something –

Jen

I knew it.

Nora

Me and Isa, we –

Mel

No!

Jen

Mel, don't stop her.

Nora

No, it's not like that. No.

Jen

Course not.

Nora

No, it's ... I was talking about,
about the stuff in the dig.

Jen

Oh yeah?

Nora

Yes.

Jen

You realise, if you don't tell us now,
there's no way we're gonna make
life sweet for ye.

Nora

It's nothing. We just kept some
things for ourselves.

Jen

You're a thief!

Nora

No! It's just they're just going to be
shoved away in storage anyway.

Mel

Tell me about it, my life's in a
fuckin' freight container.

Jen

Aw, Mel!

(To Nora)
Don't worry, we won't
tell anyone.

Nora

Thanks.

Jen

Let's move on. What next?

Mel

Dare or drink.

Jen

Ah! Classic. I dare yous three to
run through the servants' quarters
topless!

Mel

Child's play.

Viki gets up belligerently and starts unbuttoning her shirt. Mel follows suit.

Nora

You'd rather do that than drink?

Viki

It's your compound next time
Jen, OK?

Jen

Right you are. *(To Nora.)* What you
shaking your head for? *(Beat)* Thief.

Nora is welling up.

Oh what? You're gonna cry? Are you
a woman or a freakin' insect?

Mel

I'm actually getting cold now.

Viki

Hurry up, do you want Ms Cray to
know about your and Isa's habit?

Nora

What?

Jen

You heard the girl. *(Beat.)* Don't
think Mr Green'd like it either.

Nora takes the bottle and gulps from it.

Jen

Yeah, this isn't kindergarten; you
do at least half the bottle. It's not
that much!

*Nora gets up angrily and starts to walk off. Jen climbs onto the roof of the
changing room and begins to holler.*

Jen

Hey! Everyone! Nora Green and Is —

Nora

(Shouts)
OKaaaaaaay!

Nora downs the bottle of vodka and smashes it on the ground. She storms off.

Jen

Wooooooooooooo. Some fuckin'
spirit at last.

Mel

(Calling after her.)
Yeah, congrats Nora!

*Nora looks back confused and flushed before making for the Greens'
bungalow. Mel and Viki stretch their arms out as if flying and swoop topless
around the space, laughing. Nora stoops on her way. She falls to all fours
retching.*

End of Scene

Tamsin Flower studied Acting on Mountview Academy's postgraduate course and has a BA in Film
Studies. She has worked in the fields of youth work and disability support, and currently leads
movement groups for children with special needs. Prior to attending UEA, Tamsin worked as Assistant
to the film department of Target Entertainment and as a runner for Objective Productions. She was
shortlisted for the Young Writer Arvon Award and received an Arvon 42 Grant to further her poetry last
summer. She wrote and directed *Conversation with the Symbolists*, which was performed at the Ralph
Richardson studios in 2007.

Shey Hargreaves

The Stag

EXT. BRADGATE PARK, LEICESTERSHIRE, NOVEMBER 1256, NIGHT

Dusk in a country park in medieval England. A stone hunting lodge stands atop a wooded hill. Mist hangs over the damp trees. Birds CALL, water DRIPS.

A small river winds around the foot of the hill. Heavy bracken creates a dark tunnel over the water.

EDWARD and CALDWELL paddle downriver in a wooden dinghy. Edward is 21, gaunt, dark-haired, eyes constantly moving. CALDWELL, 44, sits in the stern. He is stocky and red-faced. He takes furtive sips from a small flask, licking his lips.

The boat glides over the water. Edward looks up at the full moon rising through the branches. He breathes in the air.

Caldwell BELCHES. The BELCH resounds throughout the bracken and the trees beyond, echoing over the water.

Edward looks back at Caldwell. Caldwell smiles, folding his arms to conceal the flask. Edward regards him, suspicious.

Edward turns back to the prow, still frowning. A clear patch on the left bank up ahead comes into view. Edward moves his oar to his right hand, and paddles towards the spot. The water GURGLES around the oar. Caldwell stows the flask inside his jacket and takes up his oar. They guide the boat into the shallows.

EXT. RIVER BANK, BRADGATE PARK

Edward and Caldwell heave their dinghy ashore, their breath misting in the air. They overturn it and cover it with bracken. They straighten up. They are each wearing a thick cloth shirt, a woollen jerkin and crude leather boots.

Edward takes a felt hat from his pocket and pulls it on. He checks his belt; knife, slingshot, stones. Caldwell takes an old, well-polished bow from his back and strings it. He bends down to pick up his quiver of arrows; the flask falls out of his inside pocket.

Edward springs forward and grabs the flask. He flings it away down the river. The two listen. There is a faint PLOP. Edward smiles; Caldwell shrugs. He HICCUPS. Edward rolls his eyes. They set off into the woods.

EXT. WOODS, BRADGATE PARK

Edward and Caldwell creep uphill. Edward's hand stays on the hilt of a long hunting knife at his belt, his eyes scouting the trees.

Edward pauses, listening. Caldwell narrowly avoids bumping into Edward's back. Edward tilts his head at a mossy boulder that juts out of the ground nearby. He and Caldwell slip behind it.

Edward leans forward to peer from behind the rock. Caldwell peeps around his elbow. Caldwell shifts for a better position; there is a quiet CLICK. The two men freeze.

The woods are still. Nothing moves.

A SCYTHING, METALLIC sound; the leafy ground moves in a sudden rush. Edward and Caldwell leap apart. They stare down at an iron mantrap, jaws now sprung together.

Edward's eyes are wide. He looks up at Caldwell. Caldwell wipes a sheen of sweat from his forehead, and smiles at Edward. Edward hesitates before turning back to the woods beyond the boulder. Caldwell looks down at the trap, no longer smiling.

Edward becomes motionless. Caldwell notices this and steps over the mantrap to crouch behind Edward once more, peeping around his elbow.

A doe stands, ears pricked, forty yards away. She has white markings around her eyes. She gazes away from them, into the woods.

Caldwell brings his bow up. Edward reaches over Caldwell's back and slides a single arrow from the quiver. Edward brings his arm down and, eyes still fixed on the doe, slots the arrow into place. Caldwell bends the bow, sighting along the arrow.

A dog BARKS in the distance, and the doe darts into the undergrowth. Caldwell relaxes his bow. Edward looks in the direction of the dog's bark, down through the woods and over the hill.

The hunting lodge stands dark.

Caldwell taps Edward on the shoulder, and sets off after the doe. Edward takes a last look at the lodge, then follows.

EXT. EDGE OF THE WOODS, BRADGATE PARK

The woods peter out into grassland. The doe moves between the trees, grazing.

Forty yards away, Edward and Caldwell steal forward.

Caldwell bends his bow. Edward takes a round stone from a pouch at his belt and slots it into the cradle of his slingshot. He and Caldwell exchange nods.

Edward fires his slingshot; the stone shoots past the doe's nose and hits a tree trunk. The doe shies away from it and takes off, bounding away over the open grass.

Caldwell sights along his arrow. The doe keeps running.

Caldwell HICCUPS, surprising himself. He misfires and his arrow whistles past the doe's flank. She dashes full pelt across the open ground, and disappears over an outcrop.

Edward sinks his head in his hands. Caldwell winces.

Edward raises his head; his eye is caught and he stares up the hill. Caldwell turns to look.

A light is shining from the top window of the hunting lodge.

The dog BARKS again, closer at hand. Edward and Caldwell turn and run, jumping over fallen logs, keeping low.

Caldwell trips on a root and falls. Edward drags him to his feet. They run headlong into a clearing.

EXT. CLEARING, BRADGATE PARK, NIGHT

They stumble to a halt. The clearing is a smooth circle of grass studded with white flowers. The moon shines down.

Edward's hand slips from its hold on the hunting knife. He looks behind him at the way they came, then back at the clearing. Caldwell smiles in wonder.

Edward peers into the dark woods across the clearing. He frowns.

A DOZEN MEN, clad in hooded black cloaks and leather riding boots, appear out of the darkness in a ring, surrounding Edward and Caldwell. Back to back, Edward and Caldwell scan the circle. There is no way out. Edward draws his knife. One man steps forward; his eyes are covered in a black cloth. Shiny, healed scar tissue stands out over his cheekbones, disappearing underneath the blindfold. He lifts a hand; the other men raise crossbows to point at Edward and Caldwell.

Edward and Caldwell drop their weapons. The Blind Man comes forward. He reaches up and finds Edward's face. He runs his hand down Edward's nose to his mouth. He places a finger against Edward's lips.

BLIND MAN
Shh.

The finger bears a ring, gold, with a ruby that glints in the moonlight.

Edward stares at the Blind Man. The Blind Man moves his finger to his own lips, and smiles. He turns away.

The Blind Man beckons. Two of the men step into the undergrowth. Edward peers after them. They pull a WOMAN upright from where she has lain slumped amongst the bushes. There is a CLINKING sound. The men bring the woman into the clearing. They drop her to the ground in front of the Blind Man.

The woman, about 30 years of age, is unkempt and dirty. Her eyes are reddened and her hands and feet are manacled. Caldwell looks at her; she has bruises on her face and a split lip.

One of the men brings out a fiddle and bow from a bag on his back. Edward stares at the instruments.

The Blind Man crouches next to the woman. He touches her swollen face. She tries not to wince. The Blind Man takes a key from his pocket, feels for the manacles and unchains her hands. The man at his side passes him the instruments; the Blind Man places the bow in the woman's right hand, the fiddle in her left. He steps back.

The woman turns her head away from him. One of the men touches the tip of his loaded crossbow against the back of her head. Her face crumples. She puts her bow down on the ground, raises her fiddle, and tunes it with shaking hands, one string at at time.

She picks up the bow and slowly draws it across the strings.

A LOW NOTE hums through the clearing. The Blind Man is still, his face turned towards the woods. The woman breaks off playing; the man standing behind her pushes his crossbow harder against her head. Edward swallows. He and Caldwell are rooted to the spot, staring. The woman begins to play again, her eyes squeezed shut.

The woman's TUNE is slow and calm. She breathes in suppressed gulps as she moves the bow back and forth over the lower strings. The Blind Man lifts his nose as though sniffing the air. The woman's MUSIC rises to high, piercing notes as it becomes a melancholy lullaby. The sounds of the wind and the rustling trees have faded; the fiddle's notes fall into a breathless silence. The music brings tears to Caldwell's eyes. Edward follows the Blind Man's sightless gaze.

A glimmer of white, far away between the trees. The LULLABY soars; as it does so, the woman lets out a sob, but keeps playing. Edward squints. The glimmer of white disappears, then returns. It is closer. As Edward watches, the glimmer resolves itself into the shape of a white stag.

The stag is large, its eyes dark and clear. It listens to the music, inquisitive. It approaches.

The stag reaches the edge of the clearing. It steps onto the grass. The Blind Man walks directly over to it. The stag holds its ground, watching him. The Blind Man reaches up and strokes its neck. The stag looks at him steadily. The MUSIC changes key, taking on an uplifting, joyful tone. The stag pricks its ears forward, still looking at the Blind Man.

As the fiddle hits the highest note of the piece, the Blind Man pulls a silver knife from his belt and sinks it into the stag's chest. The stag starts back. It stumbles and falls to its knees. The Blind Man leans over it. He presses its head to the ground. Another man holds it still by the antlers. The Blind Man cuts its throat.

He sinks down next to it. The stag twitches, its muzzle in his lap. The Blind Man grips its antlers.

The stag is still.

The woman stops playing. She drops her fiddle and bow, raising her hands to her face. She sobs. Several of the men go to where the stag lies and begin stringing it up by its feet onto a wooden pole.

The Blind Man walks over to the woman. Edward eyes his knife which lies on the ground, several feet away. Caldwell sees him looking and grips his arm. The Blind Man raises the woman to her feet. He manacles her hands, gently. He gathers the instruments from the ground with care, and passes them to the man with the bag. He pushes the woman into the arms of the man behind her. She stares back at him as she is led away.

The Blind Man turns to face Edward and Caldwell. One of the men hands the Blind Man Edward's knife. Edward watches him.

The Blind Man comes very close to Edward and Caldwell. In a swift movement, he sheathes the knife in its place at Edward's belt. Edward flinches. The Blind Man pats Edward on the cheek with exact precision. He turns away; the rest of the men have disappeared along with the stag.

The Blind Man walks away into the trees.

Edward and Caldwell stand alone in the clearing. The wind RUSTLES the leaves. Edward shivers. Caldwell puts a hand on Edward's shoulder, pushing him gently towards the trees. Edward won't move. He stares across the clearing. Caldwell follows his gaze.

The doe that they failed to shoot earlier that evening stands on the opposite edge of the clearing. She looks at them. The white markings around her eyes stand out in the dimness.

Edward reaches for his slingshot with trembling fingers. Caldwell stays his hand. The doe watches them. She is calm.

CALDWELL
Not tonight.

The doe turns and, in no particular hurry, paces away through the trees. Edward and Caldwell watch her. She fades into the dimness under the trees. She is gone.

Shey Hargreaves wrote her first play at college when she was 17. She went on to study for a BA in Drama at UEA, where she developed her playwriting and expanded into screenwriting for the first time. The Masters programme has also introduced her to writing for radio and television.

Tom O'Sullivan

Barry

This monologue is based on a real conversation with an actual 'cabbie', also named Barry, with whom I had the great fortune of sharing a terrifying journey home.

(A single light shines directly onto a round, scrubbed, wooden table casting a circular glow onto its surface from above. Outside the table top, all is dark. A figure sits just outside of the lamplight, his rotund upper body's physique just visible. He wears a white vest, stained in places. He has a few days' worth of stubble on his chin, and is nursing a double gin. He leans forward into the spot and begins to speak in a thick East Yorkshire accent.)

Barry:

So I was outside that bloody awful new Fuel nightclub place, right, and I picked up this pair of dykes. Not lookers, y'know, not great ... one on 'em had a bald head. I thought it was a bloke at first, till I saw its tits. Massive they were, straining out o' this black, shiny, leather top thing like a couple of zeppelins under a tarpaulin. *(He guffaws.)* T'other one had hair at least, but she were still a bit of a bushpig. Her face was all scrunched up – looked like a bulldog chewing wasps. Double paper bag job, if ever I saw one. They ask me if I can take 'em to Gilberdyke for under a tenner. Gilber ... dyke. I thought; for that irony love, I'd take you to fuckin' Lesbos. One of 'em told me a joke. How do you get, she says, four poofters on a bar stool? Turn it fuckin' upside down! *(He chuckles for longer, then his face turns deadly serious.)* Ever noticed how it's all right for queers to call other queers queer? Course, it's not OK when it's anyone else ... *(Amicable once more.)* Anyhow, so I'm driving 'em home and all's quiet on the Western Front. I had a suspicion they were necking a bit in the back, so I do what any other *(enunciates with effort)* 'eterosexual male would do in my position – I slow down and watch 'em doing it in me mirror. T'aint very nice though – just a bit of a stiff-jawed lip rape, really. Couple o' fucking shop winda Popeye dummies being banged together for the 'ell of it. I lose interest halfway down Spring Bank East, and concentrate on the road instead ... it was two-thirty, but you never know when some stupid cunt's gunna jump out in front of you, and then it's whoop, splat, a fucking disciplinary and a fuck off stain to clean off the windscreen.

So, whilst mindin' me own little business, what should I hear, but one of the two rug munchers saying something, real quiet like. 'Bite me'. So I turn around and the cancer-patient one with the huge knockers has 'em out and the other one has got her nipples in her teeth. Well, I wasn't gunna say anything, me bein' the gentullman I am – but then the Nazi's breathing started getting louder. It started coming in rasps like a fucking hacksaw; she sounded like she'd inhaled a fucking penny and got it caught in her fucking carpet sucker: wont fucking pretty, I can tell ya. S' things like that really put you off yer driving. So here's me, all playing the saint, saying, 'Jesus girls, can't you fucking wait till yer home before you eat each other? Ant you ad your tea or summat?' And the cheeky bitch with the red fucking hair just says: 'Oh, lighten up, cabbie.'

I turn back to the wheel. Fucking outraged I was. Outraged. This ugly bint had the fucking cheek to call me … 'Cabbie'! What the fuck am I, Dick van bastard Dyke? All down Spring Bank West the Nazi was fucking oohing and ahhing, moaning like an auld biddy in a home, with me just keeping the fuck quiet. I just get onto Ferensway, and I notice the kinky little bitch has actually drawn blood. That's fucking it for me, I tell 'em 'Put a fuckin' sheet down or do it in your own home! I don't want any fucking DNA traced back to my car when you two fucking eat each other!' Know what they said to me? Know what they fuckin' said? 'Keep quiet, and we'll suck you off at the Gipsyville roundabout layby.'

Well, that fuckin' shut me up. A sucking off's a sucking off, after all. Even if it is given to you by a fuckin' moose. 'Or wouldn't wifey like that?' they're sayin' to me, as the Nazi whore slips her hand into the other one's pants. She starts bucking and rolling around, spazzin' out like a ... well, like a spaz, an' I just say: 'Fuck wifey! I haven't in twenty years, don't see why I should start now!' And one of 'em, not sure which, slips a foot out of her shoe and starts rubbing me off, well slowly with it. So there we are, weaving side to side down Ferensway, the fuckin' 'Cabbie' with a big fuck off smile on his face, not to mention the first proper bang on I've had in decades; and Fraulein Himmler giving the redhead's cunt a four-finger salute!

Then, suddenly, I sense summat's wrong. No one's stroking my cock anymore, for one thing. And those two sluts are just laughing in the back. All sat upright and proper, laughing their fucking heads off, and they're laughing at … me. So I says to 'em, 'Why the fuck're you stopping? I ain't gunna tell anybugger!' and they laugh and laugh, me all red faced and hard-cocked, and they finally say: 'Sorry, Grandad, we only fancy girls. Or hadn't you heard?' But my knob hasn't heard. It doesn't fuckin' care whether they're queer or straight, willing or fuckin' unwilling; all it sees is six holes to choose from when it hasn't had one to scrape together before, and it likes it. My cock feels like a fuckin' iron fencepole – no, worse – this erection is pumping blood all through my body, all around my poundin' head, ripping off my entire fucking skin and shooting my bloody pride into the sky. And they start fucking kissing again, fucking horrible it is but I'm still just beggin' 'em; 'Let me have a bit o' that! Please! Look, there's a layby there, I'll just stop off and have a wank! Oh, go on, ya nasty bastuds!' And I'm fucking haggling with these two whores, haggling for their fuckin' pity, haggling for a chance to get this

Barry

poison, *(tears at his pubis)* this fucking boiling acid the fuck out of me and they're just laughing and laughing their ugly fucking mugs off.

(Pause. Barry shakes bodily and downs half of his gin.) So it's simple. I stop the car, pull them by hair and tit out of it, give 'em both a clip round the fuckin' ear, and I leave 'em half naked in a freezing, filthy fucking puddle. I get back into the car and turn around in the layby. This is fucking miles from Gilberdyke; and as I pass them again, all hard done to now, one o' them's crying, the other's just shaking and looking like she might throw up; as I pass 'em, I shout out of the window. I says 'My name's Barry – Ask for me again!' *(He chuckles, downing the gin. He leans back, out of the light, still chuckling.)* 'Ask for me again' …

(Fade to blackout.)

Tom O'Sullivan was born in Bavaria, but grew up in a small village in deepest, darkest Yorkshire. He has been studying scriptwriting for the last four years at UEA, and hopes to write for television, film and the stage. He also has a fond aspiration towards writing for video games.

Marianka Swain

Getting On

Lights up on bare stage with three plain chairs. WOMAN (smartly dressed) sits on the far stage right chair. MAN (wearing a big overcoat) glances at her and smiles. She smiles back. She takes out her phone and moves it around, trying to find signal. MAN wraps his coat tightly around himself. WOMAN looks puzzled.

MAN:

Been waiting long?

WOMAN:

Half an hour.

MAN:

Half an hour?

WOMAN:

I know.

MAN rubs his hands together.

WOMAN:

Nervous?

MAN:

What?

WOMAN:

I mean, I'm … sorry, are you –

MAN:

Running late.

WOMAN:

Oh.

MAN:

Third time this week. Not my fault,
but the boss doesn't see it that way.

WOMAN:

Oh … So … You're not –

MAN:

What?

WOMAN:

I just assumed … You work here,
don't you? Sorry, I didn't mean to –

MAN:

I don't … work here.

WOMAN:

You don't?

MAN:

Why'd you think that?

>   **WOMAN:**
> I'm not sure. Sorry.

MAN gets out a Metro. *He punches the air when he gets a hard clue, then looks at WOMAN, embarrassed.*

>   **MAN:**
> What is it with this line?

>   **WOMAN:**
> Excuse me?

>   **MAN:**
> I used to be Piccadilly, thought that was bad, but this is just taking the piss. I mean, I know we're bloody Zone 5, end of the earth ... or the Bakerloo ... but –

>   **WOMAN:**
> I'm sorry, I don't ...

>   **MAN:**
> Never mind.

Beat.

>   **WOMAN:**
> Why are you ... what are you doing here, exactly?

>   **MAN:**
> Waiting for a train, what's it look like?

WOMAN:
(PAUSE, PUZZLED, THEN SMILES)
Oh, you're being sarcastic.

MAN:
(LAUGHS)
Yeah.
(PAUSE. REALISES)
No. What?

WOMAN:
So you are here for the job.

MAN:
What job am I going to get here?
Train driver?

WOMAN:
Um ... why do you keep talking
about trains?

MAN:
Well, I'm standing on a platform
waiting for a train.

WOMAN:
Very funny.

MAN:
How is that —

WOMAN:
It's fine, if you don't want to —

MAN:
What?

WOMAN:
Never mind. I just want to be
prepared, all right?

MAN:
For what?

WOMAN:
My interview.

MAN:
Interview?

WOMAN:
Yes. For Executive PA.

MAN:
PA? Who for?

WOMAN:
Christopher Hart.

MAN:
Who?

WOMAN:
Christopher Hart? CEO? (BEAT) Just
through there?
(GESTURES STAGE RIGHT)
Where Ms HR disappeared …
(CHECKS WATCH)
… God, 25 minutes ago.

MAN:
You don't really think you're in an
office?

WOMAN:
Um, yes. Why do you –

MAN:
Great. Fucking great. Not only do I
have to stand in the bloody cold, yet
again, I get stuck with a mental.

WOMAN:
You're cold?

MAN:
Well, yeah, (MIMICS HER) what with
that lovely chill wind and
temperature of minus three, yeah
I'm feeling a bit cold.

WOMAN:
But the radiator's on.

MAN:
Right …

WOMAN:
God, what's wrong with you?

MAN:
Me? What about you? Aren't you
freezing your … you know … off in
that top?

WOMAN:
No!

MAN:
What, you a vampire or something?

(LAUGHS. STOPS)
You're not, are you?

WOMAN:

Please. Would you just … stop it. I
really want this job, and I want to
be ready, so just … just leave me
alone.

MAN:

OK …

MAN lights a cigarette.

WOMAN:

It's no smoking.

MAN:

What?

WOMAN:

(POINTING TO THE WALL)
No. Smoking.

MAN:

Oh, is that what it says?

WOMAN:

Yes.

MAN stares at her. WOMAN gets up and points.

WOMAN:

See? No. Smoking! (BEAT) What, are
you blind
(MUTTERING)
 or just retarded … NO! SMOKING!

MAN:

Quit pointing at graffiti, you nutter!

WOMAN:

But ... The sign!

MAN:

Next to the coffee machine, is it?

WOMAN:

No, it's next to the front desk.

MAN:

OK, right, listen up. This, train station, those, train tracks, where sometimes if you're bloody lucky trains come along. That, Banksy wannabe, this, platform, me, pissed-off man who happens to be a fucking crossword god. (BEAT) Jesus.

WOMAN:

But ... but ...

MAN:

(MIMICS)
But ... but ...

WOMAN:

This ... you can't really think ... It's an office! How else would you rationally explain the chairs, the desk, the filing cabinet, the carpet, the ...

MAN:

Chairs: metal station chairs,
wouldn't recommend them.
Probably catch swine flu. Desk –

WOMAN:

The chairs, they're not metal.

MAN:

Yeah, they are.

WOMAN:

Sit on one.

MAN:

What?

WOMAN:

Go on, sit on one.

MAN:

Why?

WOMAN:

Go on!

MAN sits down.

WOMAN:

See?

MAN:

What? They're metal.

WOMAN sits and bounces up and down.

WOMAN:
See? They're nice chairs, squashy
chairs, *office* chairs.

MAN moves away.

WOMAN:
Fine. Don't believe me. But no trains
are ever going to stop here because
Sutcliffe, Hart and Denham isn't on
the Bakerloo line!

Pause.

TANNOY:
Ladies and gentlemen, we apologise
for the delay. This was caused by a
technical difficulty ...

MAN:
Ha!

TANNOY:
... however, if you could make your
way to your seats, tonight's
performance of *The History Boys* will
begin in five minutes.

Pause.

MAN:
What the fuck is going on?

WOMAN:
I don't understand.

> **MAN:**
> Is this some kind of joke? Are you
> ... Is there a camera?

MAN waves his arms.

> **MAN:**
> Yeah, very good. You got me.
> (TO WOMAN)
> You with them, yeah?

> **WOMAN:**
> No. I don't ... I don't understand –

> **MAN:**
> Right, enough. You really had
> me there.

> **WOMAN:**
> Please. Can you ... Do you know
> what –

> **MAN:**
> Seriously. Some of us have jobs to
> get to.

> **WOMAN:**
> No. I've had enough.

WOMAN walks straight into the wall stage right. She stares at it in astonishment.

> **MAN:**
> Yeah, sure, walk into a wall, great
> idea.

WOMAN:

But ... there's a doorway ... I'm
sure, it's right ...

MAN:

Oh for ... Come on, you.

MAN helps her up and leads her in the opposite direction.

WOMAN:

Hey, get off ... What are you ...
Help! Someone!

They walk straight into the wall stage left.

WOMAN:

Ow!

MAN:

What the ...

WOMAN runs back to the opposite wall. MAN starts hitting his wall.

MAN:

What ... What's going on? Come
on, open up! Open fucking sesame!
Let me out!

WOMAN:

(OVERLAP)
Please, is someone there? Can you
... ? Ms Adams? Please! Someone!

TANNOY:

Ladies and gentlemen, we apologise
for the delay. This was due to

circumstances beyond our control. However, this evening's performance of *Noises Off* will begin in five minutes.

MAN:

Oi! Who's there?

WOMAN sinks down next to her wall. MAN bangs at his wall.

MAN:

Whoever's behind this, I'm going to kill you! Get it? You're dead!

WOMAN:

I'm stuck here. This is it. I'm spending the rest of my life in a stupid office and I didn't even —

MAN:

For the last time, it's a train station!

TANNOY:

Ladies and gentlemen, we apologise for the slight delay and any inconvenience this may have caused.

MAN:

Yeah, what now? Waiting for fucking Godot?

TANNOY:

This evening's performance of *Waiting for Godot* will begin in five minutes.

MAN:

Oh, hey, it can hear me. Mate! Hey, can you … Come on, let us out of here, will you? (PAUSE) Hello?

WOMAN:

Oh God …

MAN:

Hello?

WOMAN:

Oh God … Oh God …

MAN:

I'm dreaming. That's it. Or someone … slipped me something. Must be. Either that or I'm going mad. Do I look mad to you?

WOMAN:

Yes!

MAN:

Oh, whatever, you're completely fucking … (BEAT) Hello?

WOMAN:

This is just … this can't be happening, not again. Cutbacks, or losing the freelance budget, or too much experience, or not enough, or –

MAN:

Give it a rest, will you?

WOMAN:

Why me? What is it? I must be cursed, or …

MAN:

Hello? Reality check?

WOMAN:

Reality?

MAN:

Yeah, OK, bad choice of words, but could you stop thinking about yourself for just one minute?

WOMAN:

Excuse me?

MAN:

Hole? No doors?

WOMAN:

This isn't happening.

MAN:

Yeah, that's one way to deal with it.

WOMAN:

What's the other?

TANNOY:

Ladies and gentlemen, we apologise for the delay. This evening's performance of *War Horse* will resume in five minutes.

MAN:

Come on, open up! Let me out!
(BEAT) I know, I know there's an exit
there, I know, I know ...

MAN slams at the wall with his shoulder.

MAN:

Shit!

WOMAN:

I'm going to die here. I'm going to
die in a shabby outer office with
beige carpets.

*WOMAN starts to cry. MAN sighs and goes over to her. He pats her shoulder
awkwardly.*

MAN:

There, there. (BEAT) Hey, look on the
bright side. At least that voice has
stopped.

TANNOY:

Ladies and gentlemen, we apologise
for the delay ...

MAN yells in frustration.

TANNOY:

Tonight's performance of *Mamma
Mia* will begin in five minutes.

MAN:

Oh, fuck off!

WOMAN:

Our father, which art in heaven ...

MAN:

Yeah, great, start praying.

WOMAN:

... hallowed be thy name. Thy kingdom come, thy will be done ...

MAN:

That's nice and all, but it's not going to help.

WOMAN:

... on earth as it is in heaven. Give us this day our daily bread. Forgive us our trespasses ...

MAN:

We really are doomed, aren't we?

TANNOY:

Ladies and gentlemen, we apologise for the delay ...

TANNOY 2:

Ladies and gentlemen, we apologise for the delay ...

MAN:

Oh, it's brought a friend along.

TANNOY:

This evening's performance ...

TANNOY 2:

This evening's performance ...

TANNOY:

... of *Romeo and Juliet* ...

TANNOY 2:

... of *Private Lives* ...

TANNOY:

... will begin in five minutes.

TANNOY 2:

... will resume in five minutes.

WOMAN:

Our father, which art in heaven ...

MAN:

Stop that!

WOMAN:

... hallowed be thy name ...

MAN:

Look, the only thing ... up there, is
some bastard, having a laugh, and
... Just stop it!

WOMAN:

... thy kingdom come ...

MAN:

Shut up!

MAN slaps her. WOMAN gasps. MAN retreats to his wall. TANNOYS continue in overlap.

TANNOY:

Ladies and gentlemen, we apologise
for the delay. This evening's
performance of *The Dumb Waiter*
will begin in five minutes.

TANNOY 2:

(OVERLAP)
Ladies and gentlemen, we apologise
for the delay. This evening's
performance of *Glengarry Glen Ross*
will begin in five minutes.

TANNOY:

(OVERLAP)
Ladies and gentlemen, we apologise
for the delay. This evening's
performance of *No Exit* will resume
in five minutes.

TANNOY 2:

(OVERLAP)
Ladies and gentlemen, we apologise
for the delay. This evening's
performance of *Endgame* will begin
in five minutes.

TANNOY:

(OVERLAP)
Ladies and gentlemen, we apologise
for the delay. This evening's
performance of *Happy Days* will
resume in five minutes.

TANNOY 2:

(OVERLAP)

Ladies and gentlemen, we apologise for the delay. This evening's performance of *Getting On* will begin in five minutes.

Beat.

MAN:

OK. There must be a way out. We got in, didn't we?

WOMAN:

Yes, but –

MAN:

So we can get out. There's a doorway here. I can see it. I walked through it. I know it's here. Simple, right?

Sudden blackout.

WOMAN:

Oh God!

MAN:

It's OK ...

WOMAN:

Where are you?

MAN:

Right here.

> **WOMAN:**
> Where?

> **MAN:**
> By the exit.

> **WOMAN:**
> What exit?

> **MAN:**
> I'm coming towards you. Don't
> move.

Mozart's Eine Kleine Nachtmusik *starts playing over the tannoy.*

> **MAN:**
> Oh great. BT hold music. I hate this.
> Don't you? (BEAT) Hello? (BEAT)
> Hello? (BEAT) Hey, this isn't funny.
> Are you OK?

The music gets louder.

> **MAN:**
> Oh great. Fucking great. HELLO?
> Somebody please ... HELLO! HELP!

The lights come up slightly to reveal that he is now alone onstage.

> **MAN:**
> Hey, where did you ... Somebody ...
> please ... please help ... Where ...
> where is she? HELLO?

The music gets louder and louder. MAN collapses. Music suddenly stops.

MAN:

Thank you.

Beat.

WOMAN:

(OVER TANNOY)
Hello.

MAN:

Hello? Hey, where are you? Where
... can you see me? (WAVES HIS
ARMS) How d'you get out? Is there
... a door? (BEAT) Hello? (PAUSE)
Where did you go?

WOMAN:

Not far, Jim.

MAN:

Then where ... Wait, how d'you
know my name? (BEAT) What's
going on?

Long, LONG pause.

WOMAN:

I got the job.

Slow fade blackout.

Marianka Swain read English at Oxford in 2003-6 and completed UEA's Scriptwriting MA in 2010-11. She has taken part in young writers' programmes at the Gate and Soho theatres, and her achievements include having a short story published by Piccadilly Press and winning the 2004 Oxford New Writing Festival with her play *Under My Skin*.

Joe Wright

Something That's Green
A Radio Comedy Drama

1. INT. PRESS CONFERENCE (FLASHBACK)

(THE EXCITED MURMURING OF A CROWD OF PEOPLE. SUDDENLY A HUSH DESCENDS OVER THEM)

> **ANNOUNCER**
> Ladies and gentlemen, would you
> please welcome our keynote
> speaker, the leading light of science
> in the twenty-first century – Dr
> Peter Van Lee!

(TUMULTUOUS APPLAUSE AND CHEERS. MUSIC PLAYS: TCHAIKOVSKY'S *WALTZ OF THE FLOWERS*)

> **VAN LEE**
> Thank you, thank you very much.

> **MALE VOICE**
> You're an inspiration to us all!

> **VAN LEE**
> Thank you all for coming.

(THE CROWD FALLS QUIET)

> **VAN LEE (CONT'D)**
> Ladies and gentlemen. What I've come to show you today marks a monumental turning point not only in molecular biology, but in the history of humanity. For many years I worked tirelessly at the forefront of science, whilst other men took the plaudits for my efforts –

(THE CROWD BOO AND JEER)

> **FEMALE VOICE**
> Leeches!

> **VAN LEE (CONT'D)**
> But I have not come here to chastise them. I have come to appeal to them, to open their eyes to the truth that I shall now uncover. A truth that will change the world forever!

(MORE CHEERING)

> **VAN LEE (CONT'D)**
> Since the dawn of our existence, man has searched the skies and beyond for beings of similar intelligence to our own. Alien lifeforms from a distant galaxy, messages sent from across the cosmos ... we wanted to believe that there were others just like us: sentient,

(MORE CHEERING)

> wise and powerful, with whom we can share in the wonders of the universe. In all that time, our search has been fruitless. But today, ladies and gentlemen, today I can declare – it is fruitless no more!

(RAPTUROUS CHEERING AND APPLAUSE)

> ### VAN LEE (CONT'D)
> We were so busy exploring the heavens that we did not think to look where we stood. The mightiest discovery in biological history lay in wait at our feet, and all we had to do was bend down and see it!

(LAUGHTER FROM THE CROWD)

> ### ELLEN
> Get to the point, Peter. You're teasing them all.

> ### VAN LEE
> You're quite right, my dear. Well ladies and gentlemen, we come now to the main point of my announcement: what we are to do with this discovery. For you see, these beings need help if they are to reach out to the rest of the earth. And they must be. They must be allowed to meet with humanity, and it is I who must give them that chance.

> **MALE VOICE**
> God bless you, sir!

> **VAN LEE**
> I am proud to be of service to them.
> And even more proud to do so with
> my Ellen by my side, for the sake of
> humanity, and for the sake of us all!

(MORE CHEERING. THE CROWD IS GROWING RESTLESS AND EXCITED)

> **ELLEN**
> You are a true hero, Peter. We shall
> be forever in your debt. I'm so proud
> of you.

> **VAN LEE**
> It's all for you, Ellen. It always has
> been.

(HE ADDRESSES THE PUMPED-UP CROWD)

> **VAN LEE (CONT'D)**
> And now, ladies and gentlemen: it is
> time. Enjoy the feast!

(A LOUD GUNSHOT. A BODY THUMPS TO THE FLOOR. THE CROWD EXPLODE WITH FEVERISH CRIES AND CHEERS)

2. INT. LABORATORY (PRESENT)

(A TAPE RECORDER IS BEING REWOUND. FOOTSTEPS APPROACH)

> **JOHN**
> Still here, Mike?

> **MIKE**
> Jesus!

> **JOHN**
> Relax, it's all right.

> **MIKE**
> Sorry. You made me jump.

> **JOHN**
> I'm not surprised. It's eerie in here.

> **MIKE**
> Everyone else gone?

> **JOHN**
> It's 9.30. Most of them enjoy going
> home to their families.

> **MIKE**
> I didn't know it was so late.

(THE TAPE RECORDER CLICKS TO A STOP)

> **JOHN**
> Found something?

> **MIKE**
> What? Oh, no, nothing.

> **JOHN**
> What's that?

> **MIKE**
> Just a recording I made today. Whilst
> I was looking around the place.

Y'know, to make sure I didn't miss
anything.

> **JOHN**
> Right.

(A PAUSE)

> **MIKE**
> Still no trace of this guy?

> **JOHN**
> Nothing. No CCTV from outside, no
> signs of a struggle in here. He's
> vanished.

> **MIKE**
> Who made the call?

> **JOHN**
> An old woman, lives across the road
> apparently. Said she used to see him
> come out every evening, then
> suddenly – nothing.

> **MIKE**
> You'd think his family might've
> known something. Or friends.

> **JOHN**
> Doesn't have any. There was one
> other biologist – Hart, I think his
> name was. He's the only one who'd
> spoken to him recently.

> #### MIKE
> (HASTILY)
> Did you talk to him?

> #### JOHN
> A think Alison went to see him.
> Nothing out of the ordinary,
> apparently.

> #### MIKE
> Right.

(A BEAT)

> #### MIKE (CONT'D)
> Odd, isn't it?

> #### JOHN
> At least we know there's nothing
> dangerous in here now. Forensics
> said the lab was safe, no
> contaminants or 'harmful
> specimens' as they put it.

> #### MIKE
> Well that's good.

> #### JOHN
> Mmm.

(PAUSE)

> #### JOHN (CONT'D)
> Are you all right, Mike?

>   **MIKE**
> Yes, why?

>   **JOHN**
> You seem a bit on edge.

>   **MIKE**
> Oh. Well, it's just being here,
> y'know. I never like Missing Persons
> scenes. I've always got this idea that
> they're gonna jump out at you at
> any moment.

(JOHN LAUGHS)

>   **JOHN**
> Don't worry, we've checked all the
> cupboards. You're quite safe.

(MIKE LAUGHS – A LITTLE TOO FORCEDLY)

>   **JOHN (CONT'D)**
> Anyway, we're done for the day.
> We're sealing the place up tonight,
> in case the press get wind of this.

>   **MIKE**
> Oh, right.

>   **JOHN**
> The rest of CID are off to the Crown
> if you fancy it?

>   **MIKE**
> Yeah, yeah, why not. Nice drink,
> steady the nerves and that.

> **JOHN**
> (SCEPTICALLY)
> Yes. Shall we?

> **MIKE**
> You go on ahead, I'll meet you there.

> **JOHN**
> Why?

> **MIKE**
> Oh, I want to take a couple of extra
> shots, that's all. I don't want to have
> missed anything.

> **JOHN**
> We've scoured the place, Mike. We
> won't miss anything.

> **MIKE**
> I know, but I get pedantic like that.

(BEAT)

> **MIKE (CONT'D)**
> I'll be down in a bit.

> **JOHN**
> OK.

> **MIKE**
> Get me a lager, would you?

> **JOHN**
> Sure. But get a move on.

> **MIKE**
>
> Right.

(FOOTSTEPS AS JOHN MOVES AWAY. A HEAVY DOOR SLIDES TO A CLOSE. THE LOCK CLICKS. MIKE FUMBLES IN HIS POCKET, AND DIALS A NUMBER ON A MOBILE PHONE. IT RINGS FOR A MOMENT)

> **MIKE (CONT'D)**
>
> Come on!

(A CLICK AS THE CALL IS RECEIVED)

> **MIKE (CONT'D)**
>
> The coast it clear. It's just me. And I've found something you're going to love.

Joe Wright has been passionate about creative writing since a very young age; studying English Literature and Drama at BA level and then the MA in Scriptwriting at UEA has allowed his interest to flourish. He has written scripts for all performance media, but stage writing is where he feels most at home.